The New

by Ted Rueter

Happy Birthday
Happy Easter
Happy Days
– Steve

Andrews and McMeel
A Universal Press Syndicate Company
Kansas City

 For information, write Andrews and McMeel, a Universal Press Syndicate Company, 4900 Main Street, Kansas City, Missouri 64112.

ISBN: 0-8362-0506-5

Designed by Barrie Maguire

Contents

Acknowledgments

Sincere thanks are due my agent, Jane Dystel, and my editor, Donna Martin, for bringing about another quiz book on An Important American. Once again, Beltway Bob provided invaluable information.

Introduction

Newt Gingrich is everywhere. He was offered a book contract with HarperCollins for an advance of $4.5 million. He's writing two novels. He's been on the covers of *Time* and *Newsweek*. He has his own cable television program, "The Progress Report." He has his own political organization (GOPAC), which recruits and trains Republican candidates and underwrites a think tank (the Progress and Freedom Foundation). He taught a college course, Renewing American Civilization, which was beamed by satellite to more than 150 classrooms. On December 28, 1994, he was the host for TNT's presentation of *Boys Town*.

The nation is clearly fascinated with Newt. Walter Goodman, television critic for *The New York Times*, referred to "the Gingrichizing" of America. *Atlanta Magazine* identifies Newt as "the philosopher king of the New Right Republicans." *People* magazine regards Newt as one of the most interesting personalities of 1994. *Time* called Newt "America's preeminent political leader."

Perhaps the ultimate testament to Newt's status is the respect paid him by extraterrestrials. The lead headline of the *Weekly World News* of February 28, 1995, screamed, "Space Alien Meets With Newt Gingrich! 2-Hour Summit With Speaker of the House Will Change World! Secret Service Photo Captures Astonishing Encounter!" Bob Dole, who attended the intergalactic summit, said, "I'm not at liberty to say what we discussed but I can say it was one of the most productive meetings with an extraterrestrial we've ever had." Newt's press secretary, Tony Blankley, characterized the meeting as "very intense." The alien, who is looking for a strong leader on Earth with whom his planet could cooperate, met previously with George Bush, Bill Clinton, Ross Perot, and Rush Limbaugh.

The questions in this book concern the temporal, not the extraterrestrial. This book contains 175 multiple-choice questions on Newt Gingrich, organized into seven chapters. The questions concern such topics as:

—how Newt met his first wife
—why Newt divorced his first wife
—what book Newt recommends for those wishing to understand government
—the sex scenes in Newt's forthcoming novel
—what he called George Bush in his novel
—what Newt said about the White House staff
—what Newt's *Contract With America* calls orphanages
—what Newt called the Clinton administration
—who Newt thinks are "totally weird, totally bizarre"
—why editorial cartoonists enjoy drawing Newt
—how Newt characterized Bob Dole
—what Newt said about Bill and Hillary
—what bumper sticker Newt's opponent used in the 1994 election
—what Newt thinks is one of the major problems facing the Republican Party
—what Newt's goal in life is
—what Democrats call Newt
—what Newt called then–Speaker of the House Tip O'Neill
—why Newt thinks the Democratic platform resembles Woody Allen's affair with Mia Farrow's adopted daughter
—how Newt deals with criticism from the media

Clearly, we are entering the Age of Newt. No responsible person should be without this book.

I. THE PERSONAL NEWT

Newt Gingrich began life as Newton LeRoy McPherson on June 17, 1943, in Harrisburg, Pennsylvania. Newt's mother, sixteen-year-old Kathleen Daugherty, married nineteen-year-old Newton C. McPherson, a garage mechanic. According to Newt's mom, "We were married on a Saturday and I left him on a Tuesday. I got Newtie in those three days."

Three years later, Newt's mom married Bob Gingrich, a career army man, who adopted Newt. As a child, Newt lived with his parents in Kansas, France, Germany, and Georgia. Newt's mother was "very sweet and a little bit scatterbrained" and his stepfather was a "scary," distant authority figure, according to one of Newt's childhood friends.

Newt characterizes his childhood as "a great adventure. It was neat." As a teenager, Newt visited the World War I battlefield at Verdun, France. Experiencing an epiphany, he decided on the spot to forgo his plans to study paleontology and instead to change the world. He told childhood friends that he would eventually run for Congress and save civilization. "I was pretty weird as a kid," he concedes.

In 1962, as a college sophomore, Newt married Jackie Battley. The marriage produced two daughters, Kathy and Jacqueline. After nineteen years, the marriage collapsed, under very contentious circumstances. In October 1989, as part of the divorce proceedings, Jackie charged that Newt had "failed and refused to voluntarily provide reasonable support for herself and her children." In court documents, she alleged that Newt had not maintained payments on a $100,000 life insurance policy, and that he "failed to pay alimony on a timely basis." Newt's defense: he misunderstood what day of the month the payments were due.

Newt had this to say about his first marriage: "We had been going through counseling in the 1970s. It didn't work. I mean you go through life and sometimes things happen." As for allegations that he had engaged in extramarital relationships, Newt said, "In the 1970s, things happened—period. That's the most I'd ever say."

In 1982, Newt married Marianne Ginther. She said in 1989 that their marriage had been "off and on for some time," and that "you get married to get married, not because you want to 'change the world.' We can do that without being married." Gingrich, ever calculating, estimated that the union had a 53-to-47 shot of lasting. (To this point, it has.) In 1990, Newt conceded that his wife "has no interest in being married to the Whip. She'd like to be married to Newt. And sometimes we have a very difficult time transitioning back and forth."

Part of the personal Newt is Newt the churchgoer. Newt was raised a Lutheran, but became a Baptist. As a graduate student at Tulane University, Newt was baptized by immersion by Rev. G. Avery Lee of the St. Charles Avenue Baptist Church. Years later, Rev. Lee commented, "Perhaps I didn't hold him under long enough." According to friends, Newt does not belong to a church in Washington.

Newt's life seems to be a bundle of contradictions. In the words of Dale Russakoff of *The Washington Post*, "He was born fatherless to a teenage mother. He married against his adoptive father's wishes and later underwent a bitter divorce. While promoting family values, he remains close to a daughter who vocally supports abortion rights and a half sister who is gay. As he has said, 'I know life can be complicated.'"

Newt's life in Washington appears to be rather spartan, and he rarely ventures beyond Capitol Hill. He lives in a one-bedroom apartment across the street from the capitol. Each weekday, he rises at

6:00 to take an hour-long walk on the Mall. (He also manages to fit in a few hours of swimming at the House pool.) Breakfast usually consists of black coffee at his desk, possibly with a banana and low-fat yogurt. He likes to hang out at Head's, Bullfeathers, and the Irish Times (all on Capitol Hill), and he catches his movies at Union Station. His favorite literary establishment is Trover Bookstore, about three blocks from his apartment, where he likes to pick up biographies, science fiction, and action spy novels (especially ones by Tom Clancy).

Everyone seems to love Newt—or at least playing with his name. Just like Madonna and Cher, Newt has achieved one-name status. Commentators refer to "The Newt Right," "Newtonian leadership," "Speaker Newt," and "Mr. Newt." Newt's congressional district is known as "Newt's Neighborhood," and his advisers are known as "Newtoids." "Newt-Wave Conservatives" who support the "Newt Testament" and the "Newt Deal" are experiencing "Newt-o-Mania," while the Republican Congress likes to "Newter" President Clinton's proposals. The nation's first presidential primary is held in "Newt Hampshire." Newt frequently dishes out "Newtisms" and "Newtwit." Information superhighway travelers are on the "InterNewt." For those who oppose Newt, "No Newt is Good Newt." Those who can't make up their mind on Newt are "Newtral." Upon his eventual departure, some will lament, "Newtie, we hardly Newt ye."

The questions in this chapter concern Newt's record of military service, what his friends have to say about him, what his mother calls him, his first wedding, why he dumped his first wife, and his relationship with his stepfather. Start getting used to the Newt world!

1. What is Newt's record of military service?

a. He avoided the draft by renouncing his American citizenship and fleeing to Brazil.

b. He served in the Georgia National Guard.

c. He was given a dishonorable discharge for beating up thirteen guys named Al.

d. He got student deferments, and then was excused because he had two children.

e. He volunteered, but was rejected because his head was too big.

2. How did Newt meet his first wife?

a. She was his high school math teacher.

b. They were both contestants on "Wheel of Fortune."

c. He caught her on the rebound after a torrid affair with Bill Clinton.

d. He ordered her from an Asian catalog.

e. She responded to his personal ad in *Young Republican Lovers* magazine.

3. Upon arriving at Baker High School in Columbus, Georgia, how did Newt create an instant impression on his classmates?

a. The first day of school, he wore purple-and-orange-checkered bell-bottoms.

b. He was the local sales representative for the Pet Rock Foundation.

c. He dug a ditch in the football field and started rolling around like a piglet.

d. He passed out leaflets charging that American high schools were nothing but "subsidized dating."

e. He regularly thrust his hand into the air and announced, "Question here!"

4. Friends of Newt have made which of the following statements about him:

a. "I don't know whether the ambitious bastard came before the visionary, or whether he's a visionary, but he realizes you have to be tough to get where you need to be."

b. "Newt uses people and then discards them as useless. He's like a leech. He really is a man with no conscience. He just doesn't seem to care who he hurts or why."

c. "You can't imagine how quickly power went to his head."

d. "The important thing you have to understand about Newt Gingrich is that he is amoral. There isn't any right or wrong, there isn't any conservative or liberal. There's only what will work best for Newt Gingrich."

e. "He's probably one of the most dangerous people for the future of this country that you can possibly imagine. He's Richard Nixon, glib. It doesn't matter how much good I do the rest of my life, I can't ever outweigh the evil that I've caused by helping him be elected to Congress."

f. "Newt's like a bully. Remember when you're kids and there's always some tough-talking little kid, and when somebody stands up to him he caves in? Newt's never had anybody stand up to him. Newt's scenario is always: 'We're talking the truth, and you're playing dirty.'"

g. "Newt has problems with interpersonal relations. I tell him that every day."

5. What is noteworthy about Newt's half sister?

a. She actually likes Newt.

b. She's an out-of-the-closet lesbian.

c. She's always called Newt "The Newtmeister."

d. She's a counterculture Rodhamite.

e. She once dated Rush Limbaugh.

6. What did Newt's first wife, Jackie, say to the people of First Baptist Church in Carrollton, Georgia, as her marriage to Newt was disintegrating?

a. "He's really an Episcopalian anyway. He became a Baptist just to get elected."

b. "Hell is too good for him."

c. "The devil has taken his heart."

d. "I hope he turns into a pillar of salt."

e. "May Socks use his grave as a litter box."

7. Why did Newt dump his first wife?

- **a.** "She refused to dress up like a Dallas Cowboy cheerleader."
- **b.** "I could never get her to call me 'Howard.'"
- **c.** "She failed to bear me any sons."
- **d.** "She was onto me."
- **e.** "She's not young enough or pretty enough to be the wife of a president. And besides, she has cancer."

8. What was one of the formative events in Newt's life?

- **a.** Spending his eighteenth birthday in an orphanage.
- **b.** Losing his virginity to his high school math teacher.
- **c.** At age nine, going to see John Wayne's *The Sands of Iwo Jima* four times in one day.
- **d.** Being told by his parents that Democrats don't have mothers.
- **e.** Being mugged by a weirdo in New York who demanded to know, "What's the frequency, Kenneth?"

9. What was notable about Newt's first wedding?

a. When the minister asked Newt to say "I do," he made his beloved sign a ten-point contract.

b. His adoptive father refused to attend, protesting the fact that Newt was only nineteen and the bride was seven years older.

c. Pearl Bailey sang "Here Comes the Bride," accompanied by Paul Shaffer.

d. At the reception, Newt got mad and called his wife a bitch.

e. Newt made his bride promise that they'd place their firstborn in an orphanage.

10. What does Newt's mother call him?

a. "Nutty"

b. "Mr. Newt"

c. "giraffe hunter"

d. "Newtball"

e. "Newtie"

11. According to former congressman Vin Weber, how did Newt describe his father?

a. "a sensitive New Age guy"

b. "a white gang-banger"

c. "a large, brawling man who would get into fights. Newt was proud that that was his background. He liked knowing that he's combative and confrontational by nature."

d. "a hard-core socialist Jimmy Carter wimp"

e. "a caring, nurturing soul. Newt got his warm, compassionate nature from him."

12. According to Newt, "my uncle . . . taught me to smile at __________ on the television and to turn __________ off."

a. Howdy Doodie; Walter Cronkite

b. the Three Stooges; 'Gilligan's Island'

c. teenage girls; 'All-Star Wrestling'

d. Dwight Eisenhower; Adlai Stevenson

e. 'I Love Lucy'; Milton Berle

13. How did Newt go about wooing his first wife?

a. He showed up at her house, knocked on the door, and announced, "I'm here!"

b. He gave her a postcard of the White House and said, "Wanna live there with me?"

c. He told her, "I get invited to a lot of receptions and parties. If you marry me, you wouldn't have to do much cooking."

d. He bragged that he had access to Clarence Thomas's collection of pornographic videotapes.

e. He offered to make her his Whip.

14. What kind of car does Newt drive?

a. a 1995 black Cadillac

b. an El Camino pickup, with Astroturf in the back

c. a Rolls Royce, driven by the guy who played Ralph the Doorman on "The Jeffersons"

d. a beat-up Volkswagen, covered with "Flower Power" bumper stickers

e. a 1967 Ford Mustang

15. What was the nickname of Newt's biological father?

- **a.** "Dadorama"
- **b.** "Gingrichitis"
- **c.** "Big Newt"
- **d.** "lizard man"
- **e.** "blowhard's dad"

16. What did Newt do when his biological father was gravely ill with cancer in 1972?

- **a.** He inquired if he was still in the will.
- **b.** He sent a "Get Well Soon" card.
- **c.** He reminded his dad that he still owed him twenty-five dollars from that time in Las Vegas when he lost his wallet.
- **d.** He harshly lectured him not to feel sorry for himself.
- **e.** He told him he never really liked him.

17. Newt's mom, Kathleen Gingrich, and Bill Clinton's late mom, Virginia Kelley, seem to have a number of things in common. For each entry, indicate if it applies to Gingrich's mom or Clinton's mom.

a. nickname: "Kit"

b. nickname: "Dado"

c. age at first marriage: twenty

d. age at first marriage: sixteen

e. length of first marriage: two years, eight months (widowed)

f. length of first marriage: three days (divorced)

g. total marriages: two

h. total marriages: five (to four men)

18. In 1984, a reporter for *Mother Jones* asked Newt whether his private life had been consistent with what he said in public. What did Newt say?

a. "What's that got to do with the price of tea in China?"

b. "Consistency is the hobgoblin of small minds."

c. "Is yours?"

d. "No."

e. "Hypocrisy is one of the finest traditions of American politics."

19. What did Newt's adoptive father say after Newt was sworn in as Speaker?

- **a.** "I can't believe he's amounted to anything. He was the dumbest, laziest kid I ever saw."
- **b.** "That boy never stops talking."
- **c.** "He can't wait to take my Social Security away."
- **d.** "Does anybody actually like him, or are they just afraid of him?"
- **e.** "After the third standing ovation, it gets a little old."

20. According to his adoptive father, as a boy Newt "always tried to walk like __________."

- **a.** John Wayne
- **b.** the Rainbow Grill Peacock Girls
- **c.** Deion Sanders
- **d.** the Supremes
- **e.** Ricki Lake

21. How did Newt respond upon hearing that a Utah newspaper had reported that he kissed a "bimbo" on the street in Washington?

- **a.** "What are you saying—that only Bill Clinton is allowed to kiss bimbos?"
- **b.** "That was no bimbo. That was my wife."
- **c.** "I've got an open marriage. Leave me alone, you hippie freak!"
- **d.** "Hey—at least it wasn't Gennifer Flowers or Paula Jones!"
- **e.** "Those sexist pigs! No woman should be called a 'bimbo'! I'm reporting them to the NOW gang!"

22. How did Newt describe his relationship with his stepfather?

- **a.** "Father never knew best."
- **b.** "He was no Ward Cleaver."
- **c.** "It was a classic psychodrama."
- **d.** "Oedipus had nothing on me."
- **e.** "Dear old Dad he wasn't."

23. Which of the following people is considered to be a "Gingrich Guru"?

a. Anthony Robbins, the guy who walks on hot coals

b. Barbara DeAngelis, the best-selling relationships expert who's been married five times

c. John-Paul Roger, the "Mystical Traveler Consciousness"

d. Stephen R. Covey, author of *The Seven Habits of Highly Effective People*

e. Leo Buscaglia, "Dr. Love," who taught Newt how to be warm and caring

24. According to *Washington Post* reporters Dale Russakoff and Dan Balz, "To understand Newt Gingrich, one must enter the realm of ________."

a. the absurd

b. The Twilight Zone

c. dungeons and dragons

d. his motivational audiotapes

e. abnormal psychology

25. According to Newt's mom, what did Newt call Hillary Clinton?

- **a.** "the smartest woman to ever walk the face of the earth"
- **b.** "Mommy"
- **c.** "Princess President"
- **d.** "the Wicked Witch of the White House"
- **e.** "a bitch"

II. Professor Newt/Author Newt

Newt Gingrich is clearly a man of letters. He writes novels and textbooks, he teaches college classes, and he passes out reading lists to his political supporters. Newt is attempting to be America's latest successful professor-turned-politician, à la Woodrow Wilson and Daniel Patrick Moynihan. He once called himself "born to teach."

Newt attended Emory University in Atlanta, where he majored in history. He managed an unsuccessful Republican congressional campaign in north Georgia, and he founded the campus Young Republicans club. A chum from high school, Linda Tilton, recalls, "Newt was the only person I knew who had multiple phone lines coming into his apartment when he was essentially a kid. He'd frequently be talking politics with two people at once, running from one phone to another to tell each person what the other was saying."

It was then off to graduate school. While he dreamed of going to an Ivy League university, he settled for Tulane in New Orleans. By age twenty-seven, Ph.D. in hand, Newt accepted an assistant professorship at West Georgia College in Carrollton, Georgia.

Newt was a big-time activist at the West Georgia campus. One year after arriving, he applied for the chairmanship of the history department, but was turned down. One year after that, he sought the presidency of the college, but was again rejected.

Newt was reportedly a popular figure on campus. His classes were exciting and unorthodox, and he loved being the center of attention. His annual pig roasts attracted big crowds.

Speaking of his experiences at West Georgia College, Newt said, "I decided very early that I was never going to get tenure, that I was going to be a politician. I was tempted to apply for tenure after I lost [for Congress] twice. I went to see the dean, who was a good friend, who always supported me politically, and he said, 'Run for office—you're not going to get tenure under any circumstances. You've spent four years campaigning; you can't turn now and say 'Let me get back on track.'"

Even as Speaker, Newt remains the professor. In the winter of 1995, he taught a twenty-hour lecture course, Renewing American Civilization, at Reinhart College, a tiny private school in the Georgia mountains. The course was broadcast on National Empowerment Television, with audio- and videotapes on sale.

Before taking his class to Reinhart College, Newt taught at Kennesaw College in Marietta, Georgia. He had to move his base because the Georgia Board of Regents passed a rule, specifically designed for him, that no elected official could teach a course at a Georgia public university.

While at Kennesaw, Newt met Christina Jeffrey, a political science professor. As Speaker, Newt hired Jeffrey as House historian, but was forced to fire her after it was revealed that she had urged the rejection of a federal educational grant because it did not give proper credence to Nazism. She wrote, "The Nazi point of view, however unpopular, is still a point of view and it is not represented. Nor is that of the Ku Klux Klan."

Newt has also faced controversy as an author. In December 1994, he was offered a $4.5 million book contract with HarperCollins. Critics charged that Newt was cashing in on public service, and that he was subject to a conflict of interest, since Australian native Rupert Murdoch—owner of HarperCollins—had regulatory issues before Congress. After the controversy erupted (with even Bob Dole questioning the deal), Newt returned all but one dollar of the advance. Defending the propriety of the deal, Newt said, "Conservative books sell. I can't help it if liberal books don't sell."

Humorists have commented on Newt's predicament. Los Angeles comedian Tony Peyser observed that the main difference between the two political parties is that "Republicans accuse President Clinton of *making* improper advances, and Democrats accuse Newt Gingrich of *taking* improper advances."

This was not Newt's first controversial book deal. In 1984, Newt and his wife, Marianne, wrote *Window of Opportunity*, which outlined Newt's futuristic policy proposals. To promote the book, they raised more than $100,000 from Republican political activists and businesspeople, who formed a limited partnership. The money went toward advertisements for the book (which presumably increased sales and thereby increased royalties) and a remuneration of $10,000 to Marianne for her work as "general partner." According to *The Washington Post*, the deal, organized by a local developer, "was structured as a tax shelter with the ironic result that the government paid subsidies in the form of tax breaks to wealthy backers of a standard-bearer for smaller government."

Newt's *first* questionable book deal took place in 1977. After having lost two races for Congress, Newt received $13,000 from wealthy supporters to spend the summer writing a futuristic novel (which has never been published). Newt used the money to take his family to Europe.

Newt's contributions to American literature have skyrocketed since being elected Speaker. *Three* books of Newtonian wisdom have been published: *Quotations from Speaker Newt* (with a red cover), *Newtisms: The Wit and Wisdom of Newt Gingrich*, and *Newtwit! The Wit and Wisdom of Newt Gingrich.* Also, Newt's *Contract With America: The Bold Plan by Rep. Newt Gingrich, Rep. Dick Armey, and the House Republicans to Change the Nation* hit #2 on the *New York Times* best-seller list (tied with Jerry Seinfeld's *Seinlanguage*). Joking about the unexpected blockbuster, Newt remarked that the American public must think it's a diet book. "Well, I guess we are putting America on a diet," he said.

This section of the quiz requires that you study up on Newt's doctoral dissertation, his nickname at West Georgia College, his novels, his college lecture series, and his recommended reading list. And the reward for a good score? Newto riche status!

26. According to Newt, why did he go to college?

- **a.** "Girls! Girls! Girls!"
- **b.** "It was either that or 'Good morning, Vietnam!'"
- **c.** "I certainly didn't want to get a job!"
- **d.** "I heard you could get loans you didn't have to pay back."
- **e.** "I went to school to go to class to get through to become an adult to run for office."

27. What was the title of Newt's doctoral dissertation in history at Tulane University?

- **a.** *Herbert Hoover: Republican Hero*
- **b.** *The History of Demagoguery in American Politics*
- **c.** *Belgian Education Policy in the Congo, 1945–1960*
- **d.** *The Institutionalization of the American Welfare State*
- **e.** *Why the 21st Century Will Be the Age of Newt*

28. What book does Newt recommend for those wishing to understand government?

a. Frans de Waal, *Chimpanzee Politics*

b. P.J. O'Rourke, *Parliament of Whores*

c. Newt Gingrich, *Window of Opportunity*

d. Hunter Thompson, *Fear and Loathing on the Campaign Trail*

e. Cynthia Heimel, *Get Your Tongue Out of My Mouth—I'm Kissing You Goodbye!*

29. According to Floyd Hoskins, Newt's office mate at West Georgia College, what did people on campus call Newt?

a. "a pain in the ass"

b. "Genghis Gingrich"

c. "Naughty Newt"

d. "Professor Gump"

e. "Mr. Truth"

30. What academic program did Newt head at West Georgia College?

- **a.** Women's Studies
- **b.** War, Militarism, and Revolution
- **c.** Secular Humanism
- **d.** Moose Watching
- **e.** Environmental Studies

31. In the first draft of his novel *1945*, what did Newt call one of his characters, Lt. George Bush?

- **a.** "Jughead"
- **b.** "goofy"
- **c.** "Beetle Bailey Bush"
- **d.** "Cornhusker"
- **e.** "meathead"

32. Which seven of the following books were on Newt's recommended-reading list for his fellow House Republicans?

- **a.** *The Rush Limbaugh Story*
- **b.** *Sex Tips for Girls*
- **c.** *Leadership and the Computer*
- **d.** *The Federalist Papers*
- **e.** *Molly Ivins Can't Say That, Can She?*
- **f.** *Democracy in America*
- **g.** *Steal This Book!*
- **h.** *Washington: The Indispensable Man*
- **i.** *The Real Anita Hill*
- **j.** *"J" is for Judgment*
- **k.** *Pearl Jam: The Illustrated Biography*
- **l.** *Creating a New Civilization: The Politics of the Third Wave*
- **m.** *Talking Back to Prozac*
- **n.** *Monster: The Autobiography of an L.A. Gang Member*
- **o.** *The Effective Executive*
- **p.** *The World According to Garp*
- **q.** *Working Without a Net: How to Survive and Thrive in Today's High-Risk World*
- **r.** *Give War a Chance*
- **s.** *Stop the Insanity!*

33. How did the publisher of Newt's novel describe the book?

a. "about as interesting as the yellow pages"

b. "liberal elite psychobabble"

c. "a series of disjointed sentences hanging together on the thinnest of plots"

d. "an alternate-history techno-thriller"

e. "Let's put it this way: he paid *us* $4.5 million to publish it."

34. Why was progress slowed on Newt's novel?

a. He didn't know how to shift paragraphs on his computer screen.

b. He couldn't convince his editor to let him make fun of Chelsea Clinton.

c. Writing a sex scene involving a pouting sex kitten made him lose his train of thought.

d. He didn't have anything to say.

e. The plot on "All My Children" got really good.

35. Where did Newt dream of going to graduate school?

a. Bentley College

b. Maharishi University

c. Princeton

d. Newton State

e. Berkeley

36. Which of the following passages is from Newt's novel?

a. "Gently Newt took Gennifer in his arms, and his wet lips plunged deeply into the twin peaks of her womanhood. His manliness growing, he stroked her firm thighs. 'Oh, Newt,' she said, her gentle fingertips caressing his thick black hair. 'I'm glad you're not such a conservative after all.'"

b. "Dave the Democrat was robbing an honest taxpayer in the middle of the night to give the money to a lazy, social engineering bureaucrat. 'Stop—you sick, pathetic, perverted liberal!' yelled Reggie the Republican. 'We must renew American civilization, and I am the man to do it!'"

c. "It was a dark and stormy night. The sky was shaking like salt on Bill Clinton's french fries. The moon cast a shadow as scary as Hillary taking over health care."

d. "Just the facts, ma'am."

e. "Suddenly the pouting sex kitten gave way to Diana the Huntress. She rolled onto him and somehow was sitting athwart his chest, her knees pinning his shoulders. 'Tell me, or I will do terrible things,' she hissed."

37. In 1977, Newt sent the first three chapters of a novel about World War III to his intellectual mentor, Alvin Toffler. What did Toffler say about Newt's draft?

a. "Have you enclosed the reading fee?"

b. "Are you trying to *cause* a war?"

c. "You are obviously better at shaking hands than writing fiction."

d. "You say you went to college?"

e. "Have you heard of spell-check?"

38. What book was Newt unable to force himself to finish?

a. *Men, Women, and Relationships*

b. *War and Peace*

c. *How to Be a Civilized Person*

d. *Ferraro: My Story*

e. *The Great Santini*

39. As a graduate student in history at Tulane, what did Newt protest?

a. the fact that the administration was barring the campus newspaper from printing nude photographs

b. the refusal of the dining personnel to wear hair nets

c. the decision by the university to have George McGovern give the commencement address

d. the failure of the student government to fulfill its campaign promise to bring the Statue of Liberty to campus

e. the hiring of a professor who admitted to having read *Das Kapital*

40. In 1990, what book was useful to Newt when he opposed President Bush's tax increase?

a. *A Hero in Spite of Himself*

b. *A Return to Love*

c. *Good Boys and Dead Girls*

d. *The Rose and the Thorn*

e. *Advice and Consent*

41. How did Professor Pierre Henri Laurent, Newt's graduate school adviser, characterize Newt's dissertation?

- **a.** "A small project for a small mind."
- **b.** "The best dissertation I have supervised in my twenty-two years as a graduate adviser."
- **c.** "It's a good little dissertation; it's nothing earth-shattering."
- **d.** "We let him have a Ph.D. just to get rid of him."
- **e.** "I really couldn't tell you. I didn't read it."

42. In his college course, Renewing American Civilization, Newt pontificated about gender roles, making which of the following statements:

- **a.** "In wartime, women have problems being in a ditch for thirty days because they get infections."
- **b.** "Men are basically little piglets. You drop them in the ditch, they roll around in it. It doesn't matter."
- **c.** "A male gets very, very frustrated sitting in a chair all the time because males are biologically driven to go out and hunt giraffes."
- **d.** "If upper-body strength matters, men win. They are both biologically stronger and they don't get pregnant."
- **e.** "Pregnancy is a period of male domination in traditional society. On the other hand, if what matters is the speed by which you can move the laptop, women are at least as fast and in some ways better."

43. In Professor Newt's view, what shapes history?

- **a.** the Book of Revelation
- **b.** testosterone
- **c.** the alignment of Venus and Mars
- **d.** technology
- **e.** the intermarriage of cousins among European royalty

44. What did Alan Brinkley, professor of history at Columbia University, say about Newt's college course?

- **a.** "If this were not Newt Gingrich, it would be meaningless pabulum."
- **b.** "Brilliant. There should be a special Nobel Prize category just for Newt."
- **c.** "No wonder Princeton turned him down."
- **d.** "Sound and fury, signifying nothing."
- **e.** "I hear he's an easy grader. Just tell him you're a Republican and you get an A."

45. In February 1995, the Democratic National Committee started a weekly newsletter devoted to Newt. What is the title of the publication?

a. *Newt Nonsense*

b. *Gingrich Gobbledygook*

c. *Neutralizing Newt*

d. *NewtGram*

e. *This Week with Newt Gingrich*

46. According to Newt, what book describes his own life story?

a. *The Greatest Story Ever Told*

b. *Lost Honor*

c. *Going Crazy: An Inquiry Into Madness*

d. *The Difficult Child*

e. *Men Who Hate Women*

47. In high school, what was the topic of a thirty-page, single-spaced report by Newt?

a. "My plan for world domination"

b. "Castration: Key to welfare reform"

c. "How to pick up girls"

d. "Why imbeciles vote Democratic"

e. "British, Soviet, and American naval power"

48. According to Weston Kosova of *The New Republic,* "the Gingrich revolution comes with a code all its own. His sentences are peppered with 'paradigms' and 'processing models,' 'systems' and 'waves.' But peel away the jargon and it's not difficult to figure out what spines face out on Gingrich's shelves. His chapbook is essentially a mind-meld of ________."

a. *Getting Even* and *Marie Antoinette*

b. *Gentleman's Quarterly* and *The Seventy-Seven Habits of Highly Ineffective People*

c. *Winning Through Intimidation* and *How to Win Friends and Influence People*

d. Edward Deming (total quality management) and Alvin Toffler *(Future Shock, The Third Wave)*, with the specter of Ronald Reagan taking a few bows in the margins

e. *The Man Who Changed the World* and *Benedict Arnold*

49. In his opening speech as House Speaker on January 4, 1995, what book did Newt "commend to you all"?

a. Marvin Olasky, *The Tragedy of American Compassion*

b. Robert James Waller, *The Bridges of Madison County*

c. O.J. Simpson, *I Want to Tell You*

d. Rosie Daley, *In the Kitchen With Rosie*

e. Li Zhisui, *The Private Life of Chairman Mao*

50. Katharine Q. Seelye of *The New York Times* describes Newt's office as follows: "The new Speaker's office is bedecked in dinosaur memorabil-ia, reflecting his long-time passion and is awaiting a Tyrannosaurus rex skull that the Smithsonian Institution plans to lend him. Between the political books on his shelves are tucked volumes like _______and_______."

a. *The Autobiography of Malcolm X* and *Bondage* by Patti Davis

b. *If I Ran the Circus* by Dr. Seuss and *The Fourth Instinct* by Arianna Huffington

c. James Patterson, *Kiss the Girls* and James Finn Garner, *Politically Correct Bedtime Stories*

d. *Zen and the Art of Motorcycle Maintenance* and *101 Ways to Avoid Reincarnation*

e. *Barney Fife's Guide to Life, Love, and Self-Defense* and *Why Women Need Chocolate*

III. CONGRESSMAN NEWT

Congressman Newt is a very busy guy: directing GOPAC (the GOP Action Committee), campaigning for fellow Republicans, giving press conferences, making speeches, hosting his own cable show, teaching a college course, and appearing on network interview programs. Newt has gone from the "brash bomb-throwing bad boy of CSPAN" to Speaker of the House. Journalists note that "FONs (Friends of Newt) are in; FOBs (Friends of Bill) are out," and that the new battle in Washington is "The Hill vs. Bill." A Newt constituent exclaimed, "He's the de facto president of the United States!"

Newt was first elected to the House in 1978, on his third try, at age thirty-five. He represents Georgia's Sixth District, which consists of suburban Atlanta. *Business Week* wrote that "the district's culture combines rugged individualism born of an agrarian past, old-fashioned religious values, and a visceral disdain for Washington—particularly President Clinton."

Newt set out to make a name for himself in the House. In 1983, he founded the Conservative Opportunity Society, devoted to a Republican takeover of the House and the promotion of conservative policies. The group met regularly to plot ways to make nusances of themselves on the House floor.

And Newt succeeded gloriously. Taking advantage of the CSPAN cameras, he frequently made one-minute speeches in which he lodged charges against Democrats—and then dared them to defend themselves. What the camera failed to show was that Newt was almost always speaking to an empty chamber. Newt also managed to force then-Speaker Jim Wright to resign because of a questionable book deal (in spite of the fact that Newt has had three questionable book deals), and he led the attack on the House banking scandal (in spite of the fact that he bounced twenty-two checks himself).

In 1986, Newt expanded his empire by taking over GOPAC. Founded in 1978 by former Delaware governor Pete duPont and twelve other Republican governors, GOPAC is attempting to build a "farm team" of local candidates. When asked by a reporter why he wouldn't disclose the names of the contributors to GOPAC, Newt responded, "Pervert! Hippie! Traitor!"

Another aspect of "Newt, Inc." is the Progress and Freedom Foundation. This group sponsored Newt's course, Renewing American Civilization, which was beamed by satellite to more than 150 classrooms across the country. Although it was avowedly nonpartisan, one of Newt's associates wrote in a fund-raising letter that the course hoped to "train, by April 1996, 200,000 citizens into a model of replacing the welfare state and reforming our government."

In 1989, Newt began his climb up the House Republican leadership. John Tower, President Bush's first nominee for secretary of defense, was rejected by the Senate. Bush then turned to Congressman Dick Cheney, the House Republican Whip. After Cheney's departure, Newt was elected Whip by a two-vote margin.

In April 1989, Newt became the subject of a House Ethics Committee probe. The ten-point complaint alleged that Newt violated House rules on outside income and gifts by receiving money to help finance two books.

In July 1989, Newt was the subject of a second ethics probe. This one charged that in 1986 and 1988, Newt took two staff members off his congressional payroll to work on his reelection campaigns and then returned them to the payroll after the election with significant (albeit temporary) increases in salary.

While Newt's electoral base now seems assured, it wasn't always so. Newt won the 1990 general election by only 974 votes, and triumphed in the 1992 Republican primary by only 980 votes.

By 1994, Newt was firmly in charge of his troops. He recruited scores of Republican congressional candidates who were loyal to him, and House Republican leader Bob Michel was retiring.

On September 27, 1994, Newt brought 367 Republican congressional candidates to Washington to sign his brainchild, the "Contract With America." The ten-point proposal, which nationalized the midterm election, called for term limits, increased defense spending, tax cuts, spending reductions, a balanced budget amendment, and welfare reform. One liberal publication, *The Nation*, called Newt's contract "post-Reagan debris." Once in office, Newt moved contract items through the House so quickly that *USA Today* called him "a rebel without a pause."

Newt has been at the center of controversy ever since the November 1994 election. On election night, he refused to speak to Peter Jennings, to protest ABC's coverage of the campaign. The day after the election, he declined to interrupt an appearance on a radio talk show to take a call from President Clinton; after getting off the air, he waited for ninety minutes before calling Clinton back.

On December 5, 1994, Newt was nominated for Speaker of the House by incoming House Republicans, to the chant of "Newt! Newt! Newt!" Representative Henry Bonilla of Texas, in a nominating speech, said that choice of Newt will "go down in history as a turning point for America. Newt Gingrich is a visionary, a believer in basic values."

On January 4, 1995, Newt was installed as the 58th Speaker of the House. The event took on the air of an inauguration; Newt was treated by the media like a copresident. As Newt took the oath of office, someone on the House floor yelled, "It's a Whole Newt World!" Many people at the Capitol wore buttons that proclaimed, "Under Newt Management."

As Speaker, Newt has faced criticism on the ethics front. Besides the book deal, Newt has been chastised for attending a $50,000-a-plate dinner for National Empowerment Television and taking taxpayer-subsidized weekend trips to teach his college class. Newt got very angry when questioned about the fact that his wife, Marianne, had accepted a $30,000-a-year job recruiting American companies to a business park in Israel. Also, it was disclosed that a lobbyist who gave $25,000 to finance Newt's college course wrote a note saying, "Newt, thanks again for the help on today's committee hearing." Also, three Democratic congressmen alleged that Newt improperly accepted as much as $200,000 worth of free TV time from a cable operator with a significant financial stake in telecommunications legislation. (Newt ultimately decided to discontinue teaching the course, due to the demands on his time.) Finally, House Democrats filed a formal complaint against Newt for using the House floor to encourage viewers to call his 800 number to order audio- and videotapes of his college lectures. Democratic Whip David Bonier noted the House "isn't the Home Shopping Network." Newt expressed shock that anyone would criticize his exercise of the First Amendment.

The questions in this chapter explore Newt's congressional career, including how he characterizes the Democratic Party, the one nice thing he had to say about President Clinton, what he said about the Susan Smith murder case in South Carolina, and what song he had the band play at his 1994 election-night victory party. And remember: try to control your Newt envy.

51. What does Newt propose for welfare reform?

a. trading welfare recipients for Cuban baseball players

b. reinstituting debtors' prisons

c. creating concentration camps for fourteen-year-old mothers

d. establishing orphanages

e. making welfare recipients pay back all the money they received, at 10 percent interest

52. What did Newt say about the Clinton White House staff?

a. "I had a senior law-enforcement official tell me that in his judgment, up to a quarter of the White House staff, when they first came in, had used drugs in the last four or five years."

b. "the finest collection of human beings since the Nuremberg trials"

c. "the diaper patrol"

d. "If Clinton's staff 'looks like America,' I'm moving to Canada."

e. "I think they all received their sex education from Joycelyn Elders."

53. What issue was Newt's first legislative priority after the 1994 election?

a. abolishing the First Amendment

b. repealing the assault rifle ban in time for giraffe season

c. eliminating Social Security

d. a constitutional amendment to allow school prayer

e. rescinding the 1964 Civil Rights Act

54. According to Newt, "The mother killing the two children in South Carolina vividly reminds every American how sick the society is getting and how much we need to change things. ______________."

a. It's almost as bad as the time I delivered divorce papers to my wife in the hospital after her cancer operation

b. Things are really bad when David Letterman's favorite show is 'Beavis and Butt-head'

c. The key is to cut the capital gains tax. That will pretty much solve everything

d. And it doesn't help matters much when a major television character has a child out of wedlock and thumbs her nose at fatherhood and families

e. The only way you get change is to vote Republican

55. What expert did Newt bring in to speak to the Republican House freshman class?

- **a.** Dr. Ruth Westheimer
- **b.** Andy Rooney
- **c.** Miss Manners
- **d.** Rush Limbaugh
- **e.** Forrest Gump

56. What does Newt's *Contract With America* call orphanages?

- **a.** "steel-plated institutions for the less fortunate"
- **b.** "Newt's Revenge"
- **c.** "absolutely free to the lucky inhabitant"
- **d.** "children's homes"
- **e.** "A lot better than a Russian gulag. Count your blessings!"

57. In an October 14, 1994, private meeting with lobbyists, what did Newt call the Clinton administration?

- **a.** "Moscow West"
- **b.** "freaks, frauds, and fellow travelers"
- **c.** "the enemy of normal Americans"
- **d.** "Weirdos! Idiots! Communists!"
- **e.** "full of sodomists, ecofreaks, and misogynists"

58. Who was Newt's opponent in the 1994 congressional elections?

- **a.** Max Bear, better known as Jethro on "The Beverly Hillbillies"
- **b.** Don Knotts, better known as Barney Fife on "The Andy Griffith Show"
- **c.** Fred Grandy, better known as Gopher on "The Love Boat"
- **d.** Ben Jones, better known as Cooter on "The Dukes of Hazzard"
- **e.** Sonny Bono, better known as Cher's former husband

59. When asked to say something nice about President Clinton, what did Newt say?

a. "He's a good guy to have a drink with. He'd be a great frat president."

b. "Can I get back to you on that?"

c. "He makes a great object of ridicule."

d. "He's got a really cute wife."

e. "I love Chelsea's hair."

60. Newt has compared being Speaker of the House to being a head coach. How did he describe his role as Minority Whip?

a. "the tackling dummy"

b. "holding a clipboard while wearing a baseball cap"

c. "an aggressive middle linebacker"

d. "the guy who dumps Gatorade on the coach's head"

e. "the goon they send in to break the quarterback's neck"

61. What campaign tactic did Newt's 1994 congressional opponent use?

- **a.** He asked voters, "Do we really want a Speaker named Newt?"
- **b.** He showed up with bloodhounds at Gingrich rallies in other districts to dramatize Newt's globe-trotting on behalf of other candidates.
- **c.** He shaved his head and promised to seek world peace by teaching transcendental meditation to all members of Congress.
- **d.** He attempted to send Newt boxes of exploding cigars.
- **e.** He challenged Newt to a duel.

62. What was one of the bumper stickers of Newt's 1994 congressional opponent?

- **a.** "Newt—Not!"
- **b.** "Boot Newt"
- **c.** "Nuke Newt"
- **d.** "Just Say No to Newt!"
- **e.** "Don't Let the Gingrinch Steal Your Christmas"

63. In 1978, Newt told a group of college Republicans, "One of the great problems in the Republican Party is that ________."

- **a.** all the good-looking babes are Democrats
- **b.** you guys are nerds
- **c.** the party is full of old ladies with blue hair
- **d.** we let in people who aren't rich
- **e.** we don't encourage you to be nasty

64. What song did Newt have the band play at his 1994 campaign victory party?

- **a.** James Brown, "I Feel Good"
- **b.** The Beatles, "Back in the USSR"
- **c.** Fleetwood Mac, "Don't Stop Thinking About Tomorrow"
- **d.** Conway Twitty, "I Don't Want To Be With Me"
- **e.** Nanci Griffith, "Say It Isn't So"
- **f.** "Happy Days Are Here Again"
- **g.** Dionne Warwick, "Promises, Promises"
- **h.** The Clash, "Cold Confusion"
- **i.** Bobby Brown, "Don't Be Cruel"
- **j.** Rush, "New World Order"
- **k.** Linda Ronstadt, "You're No Good"
- **l.** Ugly Kid Joe, "Madman"

65. What was Newt's campaign tactic in his 1978 congressional race against state senator Virginia Shapard?

a. He demanded to know why she hadn't volunteered for the army.

b. He accused her of being a lifelong thespian.

c. He ran a television ad accusing her of breaking up her family because she intended to commute between Georgia and Washington and leave her children with a nanny.

d. He marketed a bumper sticker reading: "Shapard for Congress: Why Not the Worst?"

e. When Shapard was in the middle of a speech at the Carrollton, Georgia, train station, he paid the conductor to drive the train away.

66. In 1989, Newt's political organization, GOPAC, drew up a list of 133 labels that it encouraged candidates to use to ridicule their opponents or to praise themselves. Which nine of the following negative terms were on the list?

a. sick

b. pathetic

c. perverted

d. liberal

e. weirdo

f. shallow

g. hippie freak

h. incompetent

i. liar

j. permissive

k. destructive

l. insecure

m. insensitive

n. bizarre

o. crackpot

67. In the 1980s, Newt made a name for himself by blasting Democrats on the House floor as the CSPAN cameras rolled. Newt often made a charge and then dared a Democrat to come forward to refute it. What the cameras did not show, because of their tight angle, was that Newt was speaking to an empty chamber. Tip O'Neill, then Speaker, ordered the cameras to pan the chamber, exposing the fact that no one was there. O'Neill called Newt's performance "the lowest thing I've seen in my thirty-two years of Congress." How did Newt respond?

a. He said, "What do you mean—'the lowest thing'? I've done far worse stuff than this!"

b. He sued O'Neill for character definition.

c. He said, "I'm famous!"

d. He said, "Hey, what about the times that Jimmy Carter spoke here? Those were all pretty obscene!"

e. He said, "Lowest thing he's seen in thirty-two years? Tip O'Neill hasn't been able to see in thirty-two years!"

68. According to Newt, "Democrats are the party of ________."

a. lesbians, lawyers, and leeches

b. sex, drugs, and rock and roll

c. welfare recipients, street people, minorities, and other undesirables

d. people who would rather watch *Natural Born Killers* than *Boys Town*

e. total bizarreness, total weirdness

69. To what charitable cause has Newt pledged to donate $10,000?

a. the National Rifle Association

b. Sony Bono's congressional campaign

c. the Aryan Nation

d. a privately funded network to support Big Bird and Barney

e. National Organization for Women

70. What group endorsed Newt in his 1974 congressional campaign?

a. the Georgia branch of the KKK

b. the Lesbian Alliance

c. the League of Conservation Voters

d. the Men's Rights League

e. the Philosophical Anarchists Society

71. In 1982, Newt threatened his congressional staff with a $200-a-week salary reduction for what offense?

- **a.** failing to tape his speeches for a personal archive he was establishing at West Georgia College
- **b.** failing to address him as "Mr. Future Speaker"
- **c.** failing to whistle "Hail to the Chief" whenever he entered a room
- **d.** failing to alert him immediately whenever Rupert Murdoch called.
- **e.** failing to keep his mother away from Connie Chung

72. Occasionally, Newt has earned speaking fees in excess of what House rules allow. What has he done with the extra money?

- **a.** He burned it, in an attempt to reduce inflation.
- **b.** He sent it to the Nicaraguan contras.
- **c.** He gave it to Roger Clinton, just to annoy Bill.
- **d.** He helped the Atlanta zoo buy two baby rhinoceroses, Bob and Rosie.
- **e.** He purchased 100,000 copies of Marilyn Quayle's novel.

73. Which of the following is one of Newt's legislative proposals?

- **a.** applying U.S. laws to space colonies
- **b.** requiring AIDS patients to have an "A" tattooed onto their bottoms.
- **c.** banning any reference to masturbation in high school sex education programs
- **d.** eliminating the FDA's new food labeling requirement, because "what I don't know can't hurt me"
- **e.** denying welfare benefits to anyone who can't prove that their ancestors were on the *Mayflower*

74. Congressman Newt said in 1991, "Obviously, ________ isn't the issue it used to be."

- **a.** water fluoridation
- **b.** Jimmy Carter's killer rabbit
- **c.** preventing women soldiers from developing infections
- **d.** character assassination
- **e.** anticommunism

75. What did one of Newt's campaign flyers say about his 1978 congressional opponent, Virginia Shapard?

a. "My opponent is a she. Enough said."

b. "She's a Democrat. She supports Jimmy Carter. Jimmy Carter has lust in his heart. Should we really be sending a sexual pervert to Washington?"

c. "She'd probably *welcome* a Soviet invasion of Afghanistan. At least that's what I've heard."

d. "If you like welfare cheaters, you'll love Virginia Shapard. "

e. "Apparently, Virginia believes in Santa Claus."

IV. NEWT ON NEWT

While Newt talks about a veritable plethora of subjects, one of his favorites is Newt. He's conceived of a number of identities for himself. One of them is army brat. He wrote to his Georgia constituents in 1982, "Having been an army brat, I know how exciting military life can be." He said in 1995, "You grow up an army brat named Newton and you learn about combat."

There's also Newt the self-described politician. He told *The Atlanta Journal* in 1974 that his ambition "is to be an old-time political boss in twenty years." He told *The Atlantic* in June 1993 that "I'm a creature of the House."

Newt also sees himself as happy and mellowing. He said in 1993, "I'm having fun. I'm doing everything I want to do." In 1983, Newt announced that he did not "intend to stay in politics dominated by smearing and mudslinging—a politics which has all too often been characteristic of recent years in this country." On the eve of the 1994 election, he declared that "I've been seen as a partisan, and I am a partisan. But that era is over."

Finally, there's the reflective Newt. Describing his own use of marijuana as a youth, Newt called it "a sign we were alive and in graduate school in that era." Pondering his past, Newt said in 1994, "I start with the assumption that all human beings sin and that all human beings are in fact human. . . . So all I'll say is that I've led a human life." Also in 1994, musing on his tendency to make controversial statements, Newt said, "Either I have to close down that part of my personality or I've got to learn to be more careful, more specific, about what I say."

While Newt certainly has a flattering impression of himself, the American public isn't quite so sure. A

USA Today poll in late 1994 indicated that 18 percent had a favorable view of Newt, while 26 percent had an unfavorable view. A *Time* poll in January 1995 showed that Newt had a 32 percent favorable rating, compared to 49 percent for Bob Dole and 54 percent for Bill Clinton. In a similar poll, 29 percent of respondents said that Newt had good ideas for the country, while 32 percent said he did not. Even more troubling for Newt, only 19 percent said he was "a leader you can trust," while 52 percent said he was not. A study by a Republican political consultant showed that Newt had received more negative media coverage than O.J. Simpson—who had been accused of double murder.

Perhaps part of Newt's public relations problem is his acerbic reaction to criticism. After being reprimanded for his book deal, Newt complained bitterly that his political opponents would do or say anything to malign him. Representative Jim Leach, chairman of the House Banking Committee, even wrote to President Clinton that House Republicans wouldn't support the Mexican loan guarantee legislation if Democrats didn't stop attacking Newt.

The questions in this chapter test your knowledge of Newt the man. Be prepared for close questioning on Newt's self-image, his aspirations, what he has learned, his feelings, and his behavior as a teenager. May you learn something Newt!

76. According to Newt, "Truth is, occasionally, I'm ______."

- **a.** sickened by my own arrogance
- **b.** dressed in drag
- **c.** too much in love with myself
- **d.** not very smart
- **e.** saddened by the current state of American politics. Why does everyone have to be so partisan? Why does everyone have to be so mean?

77. Soon after the 1994 elections, how did Newt describe himself?

- **a.** "a transformational figure"
- **b.** "the most dangerous man in America"
- **c.** "Frankenstein"
- **d.** "a draft-dodging, drug-using, big-mouth hypocrite"
- **e.** "Elitist! Scuzzball! Liar!"

78. According to Newt, "I think of myself as ________."

a. a very bad boy

b. a harmless little fuzzball

c. Peter Pan

d. a distinguished American

e. a player coach

79. According to Newt, "People like me are what stand between us and ____________."

a. a black criminal takeover of the United States

b. responsible government

c. the Hillarization of America

d. Auschwitz

e. giraffes running around everywhere

80. According to Newt, "I see myself representing __________."

a. middle-aged, overweight white Southern men who married their first girlfriend

b. mean-spirited white guys who can't jump

c. people who love 'The Brady Bunch'

d. the conservative wing of the postindustrial society

e. giraffe hunters and piglets

81. Which of the following is one of Newt's favorite words?

a. "nasty"

b. "war"

c. "system"

d. "demagogue"

e. "weirdo"

82. According to Newt, "I am not a ________."

a. gadfly

b. crook

c. normal American

d. follower of Barney Fag—er, Frank

e. legitimate Ph.D. Just between you, me, and Connie Chung, I sent $10 to a matchbook place

83. According to Newt, "I haven't ______________."

a. committed rape, murder, theft, or any other Democrat crime

b. ever called my mom a bitch

c. written twenty-two books that are meaningless

d. stopped making a fool of myself. I'm hopeless!

e. called any of those phone sex services. Never!

84. According to Newt, "I have an enormous __________."

a. sexual appetite

b. sense of my own importance

c. pile of debt. Student loans, credit card debt, mortgages, alimony payments, tax delinquencies—I've got them all

d. ability to B.S. I got it from being in high school debate

e. personal ambition. I want to shift the entire planet. And I'm doing it!

85. What did Newt say when asked if he was better at leveling criticism than taking it?

a. "I don't think I dish it out."

b. "Of course. I love calling people weirdos and thugs."

c. "You talking to me? You talking to me? You criticizing me? You criticizing me?"

d. "If you were raised by a mother who blew smoke in your face and called everyone a bitch, you'd be nasty, too."

e. "What's wrong with calling somebody a perverted freak? That's what everyone at the orphanage called *me!*"

86. According to Newt, "I don't use __________."

a. the N-word

b. condoms

c. either boxers or briefs

d. hair dye. The gray is perfectly natural

e. hyperbole

87. According to Newt, "I feel like ________."

a. a rolling stone

b. Archie Bunker

c. Henry Kissinger. Sometimes I wake up in the middle of the night and start speaking in this thick German accent. It's kind of scary

d. an irrepressible four-year-old

e. a rebel without a clue

88. According to Newt, "I am essentially a ________."

a. revolutionary

b. power-crazed egomaniac

c. troublemaker

d. good man gone awry

e. gray-haired, middle-aged guy who's trying to salvage the wreck of his life

89. According to Newt, "I'm an American ________."

a. hero. Why do they keep talking about *O.J.* as a hero? *I'm* the hero!

b. original. There's never been another me

c. Gaullist

d. Ho Chi Minh

e. boy. There's not an ounce of foreign blood in me

90. How does Newt describe his behavior around his wife, Marianne?

a. "I can't keep my hands off her. I'm as lustful as Jimmy Carter."

b. "She can't take me anywhere."

c. "I'm calmer, less likely to make mistakes if she's around."

d. "Why does she get so upset when I buy flowers for other women? I'm just trying to be friendly!"

e. "I don't have a wife. I have a coequal domestic associate of the opposite sex."

91. What is Newt's aspiration?

a. "to be the best darn anchorman in Minneapolis"

b. "to pay off my student loans"

c. "to get Cokie Roberts to like me"

d. "to be the leading teacher of twenty-first-century American civilization"

e. "to gather the courage to go bungee jumping"

92. In December 1994, Newt said on a television interview program, "I have learned ________."

a. that cherry pie gives me an intense sugar buzz

b. very little in my life. It's amazing that anyone takes me seriously

c. all the letters in the Greek alphabet

d. that everything I say has to be worded carefully and thought through at a level I've never experienced

e. that George Bush is a wimp

93. How did Newt describe his approach to the job of House Republican Whip?

a. "I don't count."

b. "I tell them how to vote, and they do it. It's pretty simple."

c. "After I got them free check-bouncing privileges at the House bank, they did anything for me."

d. "I let other people do the actual work. I'm too busy shooting my mouth off."

e. "I loved cracking that whip. I gave lots of people whiplash."

94. How did Newt describe himself as a teenager?

a. "My middle name was angst."

b. "Mr. Oxy-5"

c. "I'm the guy in the eighth grade who did not go across the floor and ask the girl to dance for two reasons. One is, she might say no and I'd be embarrassed; two, she might say yes and I'd have to dance."

d. "I still feel like a teenager. Dick Clark has nothing on me! I've always said that MTV is the key to renewing American civilization. And Martha Quinn—what a babe!"

e. "It was a miserable so-called life."

95. According to Newt, "I am not a _____________ person."

a. totally weird, totally bizarre

b. hormonally unbalanced

c. well-educated

d. pathologically confrontational

e. warm and generous

96. In Newt's view, "I'll do almost anything ________________."

a. to win a Republican majority in Congress

b. that Bob Dole tells me to

c. to get my mom to stop blowing smoke in my face

d. to ridicule Bill Clinton

e. to get on 'American Bandstand'

97. According to Newt, "I'm not interested in ________________."

a. girls

b. listening—just talking

c. anything Mario Cuomo has to say

d. anybody else's problems

e. preserving the status quo; I want to overthrow it

98. Newt commented in 1991, "I will not rest until ________."

- **a.** I've licked my nastiness problem
- **b.** I have transformed the landscape of American politics
- **c.** I'm more famous than Jesus Christ
- **d.** the fat lady sings
- **e.** Elvis returns

99. According to Newt, "I'd like to have ________."

- **a.** Johnnie Cochran's ability to confuse a jury
- **b.** David Letterman's teeth
- **c.** Wilt Chamberlain's sex life
- **d.** Eisenhower's humanness
- **e.** Rush Limbaugh's brain

100. In Newt's words, "I'm a hawk, but ________."

a. I'm a cheap hawk

b. that doesn't mean I wanted to be in the army

c. that's no reason to get a crew cut

d. Hillary Clinton should *not* be allowed to join the marines!

e. my IQ is still in triple digits

V. THE MEDIA AND NEWT

Newt is clearly a creature of the media. He arrived in Washington in 1979—the same year that CSPAN went on the air. His mother created a storm by telling Connie Chung what Newt thought of Hillary. Newt is always reading books, and he is trying his hand at writing. Newt once said his goal was "reshaping the entire nation through the news media," and commented that "CSPAN is more real than being there." He concedes that "my relationship with the media has been symbiotic from the beginning." He told *Vanity Fair* in July 1989, "If you're not in *The Washington Post* every day, you might as well not exist."

But we all know that Newt *does* exist. For proof, just turn to his own TV program, "The Progress Report," on National Empowerment Television. Created by conservative activist Paul Weyrich, the twenty-four-hour-a-day, Washington-based network describes itself as "must-watch television for public policy wonks and junkies, the CSPAN crowd looking for more spice and pace, and the PBS and public policy crowd looking for more real-time coverage. In short, NET is CSPAN with an attitude." (Representative Pat Schroeder described the network as "twenty-four hours of Newtspeak.") NET features such classics as "Modern War" ("the only television program devoted to the ideas that govern warfare"), "American Family" ("how real American families deal with day care dilemmas, teen violence, elder care, unemployment, choices in education, and teen sexual activity"), and "On Target With the NRA" ("the National Rifle Association presents an hour of incisive commentary from policy experts and nationally known personalities").

While Newt has his own show, he's not thrilled about appearing on other shows. In January 1995, Newt said he would stay off Sunday talk programs for a month because they are devoted to "nit-picking argument." He told journalists: "Just literally dump everything out of your PC and go back and start over."

The journalistic establishment has had some amusing things to say about Newt. In 1984, Timothy Noah of *The Washington Monthly* named Newt "Biggest Gadfly" in Congress. Walter Shapiro, White House correspondent for *Esquire*, wrote that Newt "is too smart to be simply dismissed as a cartoon right-winger." He also provided this physical description: "The gray-haired Gingrich, with his middle-aged paunch, crisp white shirt, and earnest red tie, looks like the president of the Georgia Realtors." More charitably, David Osborne, in a famed *Mother Jones* profile in November 1984, said that Newt "combines qualities rarely found in one politician: He is a brilliant speaker and debater, he is an effective guerrilla political strategist and theorist, who by the force of his ideas has begun to reshape Republican politics." Syndicated columnist William F. Buckley called Newt "a talented, streetwise Ph.D." Doonesbury cartoonist G.B. Trudeau depicts Newt as a cherry bomb, ready to explode. *New York Post* columnist Jack Newfield said that "Newt Gingrich is the Tonya Harding of politics. If he disapproves of you, he will try to break your knees."

Ironically, conservative columnist George F. Will seems to have a strong dislike of Newt. In 1995, Will called Newt "the Fourth Branch of Government." In 1990, when asked if there was a new Newt, with a less confrontational style, Will responded: "In the first place, he is young. In the second place, he is probably intellectually and emotionally younger than he is biologically. That is, he has got a certain very-young-man's effervescence." Asked if that meant that he thought Newt was maturing, Will said, "Sure, ain't we all."

The good news for Newt is that his image is improving with other media types. In late 1994, the "Conventional Wisdom" column in *Newsweek* described the "Old CW" on Newt as "obnoxious, powerless windbag." The "New CW," however, was "charming, omnipotent windbag."

The questions in this chapter concern what *The New York Times*, *The Washington Post*, *The New Republic*, *Time*, *Newsweek*, and *The New Yorker*—the "liberalmediaelite"—have to say about our Newt. For inspiration, consult the Newt Testament.

101. Fred Barnes of *The New Republic* described Newt as "the most reviled Republican in the country, seen by many Democrats and much of the press as ________________."

a. Spiro Agnew with brains

b. a man with Dan Rather's sense of humor and Dan Quayle's IQ

c. an army brat war wimp

d. a red-spotted, cold-blooded oddity with a lethal secretion

e. Joe McCarthy, Richard Nixon, and Bob Roberts rolled into one

102. According to Fred Barnes, what do Newt and Bill Clinton have in common?"

a. "They're both draft dodgers."

b. "Neither of them can balance a checkbook."

c. "They're managers who operate amidst utter chaos. Gingrich runs his personal conglomerate—House office, PAC, college program, foundation—with Clinton-like efficiency."

d. "As kids, they both loved Bullwinkle."

e. "They both have the hots for Demi Moore."

103. What did *Time* magazine call Newt?

a. "Mr. Newtoid"

b. "Elephant Man"

c. "Uncle Scrooge"

d. "Never-Nervous Newt"

e. "a kook's kook"

104. According to Kevin Phillips of *American Political Report*, Newt is "a man with ______________."

a. the conscience of Ted Bundy

b. a keen sense of his own limitations

c. a large past and a dim future

d. no move to his left. He can only go right

e. an ego of rock-star proportions

105. Kevin Phillips also wrote this about Newt and Bob Dole: "The longer Gingrich comes across as ________________, the longer Dole can continue his extraordinary emergence as the nation's new political father figure."

- **a.** someone who was raised by wolves
- **b.** a *Wayne's World* geek
- **c.** a gray-haired bimbo
- **d.** a smart-aleck with an even lower trust rating than Clinton
- **e.** Dr. Johnny Fever

106. According to Sidney Blumenthal of *The New Yorker*, Newt is "the World's Foremost Expert," with an ability to "bowl over the listener with the breadth of his encyclopedic intellect. He's ________________."

- **a.** a legend in his own mind
- **b.** clearly no Dan Quayle
- **c.** not only a futurist, a management consultant, and a theologian, but Roger Ebert
- **d.** an expert on the price of everything and the value of nothing
- **e.** almost as irritating as Jesse Jackson

107. Steve Benson, editorial cartoonist for *The Arizona Republic*, said this about the prospect of drawing cartoons of Newt: "It'll be great drawing a Speaker of the House ____________."

a. named after a lizard

b. who's exactly as fat as Rush Limbaugh

c. who makes a great Pillsbury Dough Boy

d. who does something dumb on a daily basis

e. with a really stupid name

108. According to Howard Fineman of *Newsweek*, President Clinton will "actually have to cut deals with Newt, whom most White House insiders loath. Loather-in-chief is __________."

a. Chelsea

b. Hillary

c. George Stephanopoulos

d. Al

e. Tipper

109. According to William F. Buckley, "Anyone who knows Gingrich at all knows that naïveté is no stranger to his nature. Temperamentally, Gingrich makes Jack Kemp look like _______."

a. a genius

b. an NFL quarterback

c. a hyperactive cokehead

d. a guy with a gravel-pit voice

e. an undertaker

110. What did *People* magazine call Newt in 1990?

a. "Mr. Newt"

b. "Neutron Bomb"

c. "a Southern-fried McGovernite"

d. "the most cordially detested man in Congress"

e. "as smart as Strom Thurmond, as pleasant as Jesse Helms"

111. In the words of Walter Shapiro of *Esquire*, "an ascendant Gingrich will make Clinton remember 1994 as a rerun of ______."

- **a.** 'Mayberry RFD'
- **b.** *Nightmare on Elm Street*
- **c.** 'Green Acres'
- **d.** 'Happy Days'
- **e.** *Indecent Proposal*

112. How did *New York Times* columnist Anthony Lewis describe Newt's approach to politics?

- **a.** "below-the-belt bullying"
- **b.** "cultural McCarthyism"
- **c.** "hypocrisy peppered with blind ambition"
- **d.** "slash and burn, knife and smear"
- **e.** "a kinder, gentler Speaker"

113. An editorial in *The New York Times* was head-lined, "Newt Gingrich, ________________."

- **a.** Man About Town
- **b.** Master of the Universe
- **c.** Authoritarian
- **d.** The Man in the Gray Flannel Suit
- **e.** Ugly American

114. Evoking memories of Newt's messy divorce, Mike Lubovich, editorial cartoonist for *The Atlanta Journal-Constitution*, drew a cartoon depicting Newt with party girls on either arm labeled "D.C. High Rollers" coming to see his wife in the hospital, labeled "Georgia Constituents," and announcing "I want a divorce." How did Newt respond?

- **a.** He barred reporters from that paper from his office.
- **b.** He accused the publisher of conspiring to disrupt his daughter's wedding.
- **c.** He yelled at the cartoonist, "Pervert! Pinko! Fag!"
- **d.** He called the cartoonist's wife a bitch.
- **e.** He used the money from his book deal to buy the newspaper.

115. Tony Kornheiser of *The Washington Post* calls Newt the ________________ of American politics.

- **a.** Bobby Riggs
- **b.** Gerald Ford
- **c.** Charlie Brown
- **d.** Muhammad Ali
- **e.** Khirinovsky

116. In the view of New York radio personality Don Imus, Newt can sometimes be so feral that he looks like someone who enjoys ______.

- **a.** "walking on hot coals"
- **b.** "sticking children in orphanages"
- **c.** "barbecuing roadkill"
- **d.** "shooting a squirrel with an assault rifle"
- **e.** "burning Democrats at the stake"

117. Jay Leno told the following joke: "Opening day for the 104th Congress and House Speaker Newt Gingrich __________."

- **a.** is measuring the drapes in the White House
- **b.** had a smile surgically implanted on his face
- **c.** called Senator Kassebaum a bitch
- **d.** threw out the first orphan
- **e.** is giving welfare recipients one hundred days to pack their bags

118. What advice did Rush Limbaugh offer following Newt's election as Speaker?

a. "Don't moderate anything! He's got to keep firing with both barrels!"

b. "That 'bowl-over-the-head' haircut has got to go!"

c. "Stop doing all that reading! It's a waste of time! *I'm* the only information highway you'll ever need."

d. "Don't talk about yourself all the time. Nobody likes an egomaniac!"

e. "Get yourself a radio talk show. Then you'll have real power."

119. David Rosenbaum of *The New York Times* wrote that Newt is not a __________ man.

a. "nice"

b. "weird"

c. "modest"

d. "smart"

e. "literate"

120. In the words of Al Hunt of *The Wall Street Journal*, "Newt Gingrich complaining about mean-spiritedness is like _________."

- **a.** Donald Trump complaining about poverty
- **b.** Madonna complaining about promiscuity
- **c.** Don King complaining about a bad hair day
- **d.** a New Yorker complaining about rudeness
- **e.** blow-drying your hair underwater

121. What did Molly Ivins call Newt after he was elected minority whip in 1989?

- **a.** "Whipper Boy"
- **b.** "Newt the Nightmare"
- **c.** "Big Bird"
- **d.** "this repellant little demagogue"
- **e.** "a fast-talking, power-hungry hypocrite who has cheapened political dialogue and plunged the House into partisan warfare, a man whose personal life mocks his professed concern for family values"

122. According to Walter Shapiro of *Esquire*, Newt "makes no secret of his dream to ________."

a. get his mother to shut up

b. become a multimillionaire author

c. become president of the United States

d. get Madonna to like him

e. become the happy warrior of the Republican Right

123. Newt was on the cover of *Time* magazine for November 7, 1994. What was the headline?

a. "This Guy's the New Speaker?"

b. "Has God Forsaken Us?"

c. "Mad as Hell"

d. "Saying Farewell to the Corrupt Liberal Welfare State"

e. "The New Stalin?"

124. How did Peter Osterlund, Washington correspondent for *The Baltimore Sun*, describe Newt the high school student?

- **a.** "Don Juan with wheels"
- **b.** "voted by his classmates 'most likely to know it all' "
- **c.** "a right-wing Jerry Brown"
- **d.** "pudgy and bespectled"
- **e.** "the sort of geek who would get his sideburns stuck in a jigsaw"

125. A decade ago, what did conservative newspaper columnist George Will call Newt?

- **a.** "the distinguished Dr. Gingrich"
- **b.** "a cherub with a chip on his shoulder"
- **c.** "Professor Pompous"
- **d.** "a credit to his race"
- **e.** "the worst thing that's happened to American conservatism since Robert Dornan"

VI. POLITICIANS AND NEWT

Newt is not universally loved among his fellow politicians—even Republicans. Fred Grandy, then an Iowa congressman, said of Newt, "He makes the rest of us seem kinder and gentler, and I suppose there's something to be said for that." Before Newt became Speaker, Congressman Jim Leach said, "I shudder at the thought that people judge the Republican Party by him."

Certain Democrats don't seem to care for Newt, either. Senator Sam Nunn, in January 1995, urged Newt to "strive to have a higher percentage of your thoughts remain unspoken." In 1990, a poster in a House Democratic cloakroom called for a "Newt-free Congress." During the Gulf War, the following joke was going around Washington: You find yourself alone in a room with Saddam Hussein and Newt and you have two bullets in your gun. What do you do? Shoot Newt twice.

Of course, Newt is more than capable of getting off a line or two himself. He calls his critics "fixated and pathologically disoriented." In 1976, he said that Jimmy Carter was "a conservative when he smiles, a moderate liberal when he talks, and a McGovern-Humphrey liberal when he issues detailed position papers." He accused Speaker Jim Wright of being "pro-Communist." He called the Democrats leading the Iran-contra hearings "a left-wing lynch mob." He called Jim Wright, Tip O'Neill, and Tom Foley "a trio of muggers." He blasted then–New York governor Mario Cuomo for being "the most articulate spokes-man of the pre-perestroika, Brezhnev wing of the Democratic Party." In 1992, Newt charged that Bill Clinton and Al Gore had a "pre-Gorbachev, centralized-bureaucracy vision." At the 1992 Republican National Convention, Newt said that the

Democratic Party "rejects the lessons of American history, despises the values of the American people, and denies the basic goodness of the American nation." He called Al Gore's book, *Earth in the Balance*, "nutty left-wing goo-goo stuff."

Newt's favorite target is the Clinton administration. After then–surgeon general Joycelyn Elders suggested that the nation consider drug legalization, Newt said of President Clinton, "I assume he shares her values. I assume he think it's okay." Newt also charged that many members of the Clinton White House had been drug users.

In this chapter, quiz takers will be tested on their knowledge of Newt's views on Bill and Hillary, Jim Wright, Bob Dole, Tip O'Neill, and Joycelyn Elders, as well as what his congressional colleagues have to say about him. May the Newt be with you!

126. Whom did Newt call "the best all-around politician I've ever seen"?

- **a.** Charles Barkley
- **b.** Spiro Agnew
- **c.** Bill Clinton
- **d.** S. I. Hayakawa
- **e.** George Bush

127. What did Newt call Bob Dole?

- **a.** "the guy with the bad hand"
- **b.** "Senator Doom and Gloom"
- **c.** "Comrade Compromise"
- **d.** "the tax collector for the welfare state"
- **e.** "Mr. Moderate"

128. What did Bob Dole once call Newt and his allies?

- **a.** "the young hypocrites"
- **b.** "Hitler youth"
- **c.** "the Newtists"
- **d.** "the nattering nabobs of negativism"
- **e.** "the Princes of Darkness"

129. What presidential candidate did Newt work for in 1968?

- **a.** Eugene McCarthy
- **b.** George Wallace
- **c.** Richard Nixon
- **d.** Nelson Rockefeller
- **e.** Hubert Humphrey

130. How did White House Chief of Staff Leon Panetta characterize Newt?

- **a.** "a pudgy pugilist"
- **b.** "How could a guy with a Phil Donahue haircut be so insensitive?"
- **c.** "an out-of-control radio talk show host"
- **d.** "A failed academic. Why should we take a guy from West Georgia College seriously?"
- **e.** "A pretty lousy fiction writer. That line about 'pouting sex kittens' was a real gem. Newt couldn't write his way out of a paper bag."

131. What do some Democrats call Newt?

a. "Newtron"

b. "Nerdy Newt"

c. "sex kitten"

d. "Laughable LeRoy"

e. "Fig Newton"

132. What did Newt call then–Speaker of the House Tip O'Neill?

a. "Tipster"

b. "a Boston drunk"

c. "gramps"

d. "Speaker boy"

e. "a thug"

133. How did Ben Jones, Newt's congressional opponent in 1994, describe Newt?

a. "Nazi Newt"

b. "a complete idiot"

c. "a guy with an empty head and an overflowing stomach"

d. "a dangerous man"

e. "a national joke"

134. How did Newt describe then–House Speaker Jim Wright?

a. "a Texas tyrant"

b. "a genuinely bad man"

c. "Jim Wrong"

d. "Speaker Jimbo"

e. "my first victim"

135. Soon after the 1994 elections, Newt called President Clinton a "terribly ______________."

a. bad bowler

b. smart man

c. weird fellow

d. poor excuse for a president

e. irrelevant figure

136. What did Hillary Clinton call Newt's proposal to establish orphanages?

a. "unbelievable and absurd"

b. "typical Republican lunacy"

c. "the best idea Newt's ever had"

d. "Who's going to run them—Father Duke?"

e. "What's next—solitary confinement for shoplifters?"

137. How did Newt describe Bill Clinton?

a. "Dukakis with a Southern accent"

b. "When the hell is he going to clear his throat?"

c. "He's bringing about the collapse of American civilization. He's the perfect symbol of moral decay."

d. "a wild and crazy guy"

e. "He's got the worst hair in the world."

138. How did Newt describe Ben Jones, his congressional opponent in 1994?

- **a.** "a great guy to smoke a few joints with"
- **b.** "a typical sick, pathetic, immature, corrupt liberal"
- **c.** "Someone whose favorite show is 'Married . . . With Children'— doesn't that tell you something?"
- **d.** "A guy with a lot of gall! How dare he run against me?"
- **e.** "a weird left-wing actor"

139. How did Newt describe former surgeon general Joycelyn Elders?

- **a.** "a welfare mama"
- **b.** "an overt anti-Catholic bigot"
- **c.** "an incompetent surgeon—I heard she once accidentally cut somebody's head off"
- **d.** "a woman deeply in love with herself"
- **e.** "the best that Arkansas has to offer"

140. What did Newt call Bill and Hillary?

- **a.** "fools in love"
- **b.** "Slick Willie and the Babe"
- **c.** "Julius and Ethel Rosenberg"
- **d.** "mixed nuts"
- **e.** "counterculture McGoverniks"

141. Newt has often used the words "McGovern," "McGovernite," and "McGovernick" as metaphors for social and political depravity. For each of the following items, indicate if it applies to Newt Gingrich or to George McGovern.

a. has been married to the same woman for fifty years

b. served as a fighter pilot in World War II

c. earned a Ph.D. from Northwestern University

d. is the son of a minister

e. opposed the Vietnam War

f. dumped his first wife when she had cancer

g. accepted a huge book deal immediately after coming to national prominence

h. engages in name-calling

i. avoided military service

j. admits to drug use

142. Congressman David Obey, a Wisconsin Democrat, said that sometimes he sees "the ghost of ________ in Gingrich."

a. Barry Goldwater

b. Adolf Hitler

c. Douglas MacArthur

d. Zbigniew Brzezinski

e. Joe McCarthy

143. Former congressman Mike Synar of Oklahoma, defeated for reelection in 1994, considers Newt a friend. How does he characterize Newt's behavior?

- **a.** "a court-certified pathological liar"
- **b.** "a known liar and a Simpson-case groupie"
- **c.** "a megalomaniac"
- **d.** "a control freak"
- **e.** "a normal American"

144. Barney Frank, a liberal Democratic congressman from Massachusetts, isn't too impressed with Newt. "He's got everybody scammed," said Frank. "________________."

- **a.** He's really a left-wing feminazi
- **b.** The role of Newt Gingrich is being played by George Bush's evil twin
- **c.** Newt doesn't have ideas. He has ideas about how nice it would be to have ideas
- **d.** If he's from Georgia, where's his accent? Where's his pickup truck? Where's his chewing tobacco?
- **e.** The future occurs tomorrow, not yesterday

145. What did Congressman Sonny Bono say to Newt on Newt's first day as Speaker?

a. "I got you, Gingrich."

b. "Cher's autograph is not for sale."

c. "Can I get on the Rock and Roll Committee?"

d. "But I always wore shorts when I was mayor of Palm Springs!"

e. "It's like your first hit record. You dream all your life and then it happens. And it just goes through the roof."

146. Former congressman Jack Kemp said of Newt: "He's done politically what _______ did technologically and entrepreneurially."

a. Bill Gates

b. Amelia Earhart

c. Rube Goldberg

d. Wile E. Coyote

e. Frank Lorenzo

147. Former House Speaker Jim Wright says that "At heart, Newt is _________."

a. a crook

b. a nihilist

c. a thug

d. a weirdo

e. heartless

148. At a meeting of the Democratic National Committee, Hillary Clinton said of Newt, "I don't really care what the Speaker says about me. I wish he would ____________."

a. lose some weight

b. take his mother to Miss Manners

c. run for president. Bill would cream him

d. give me an A in his class

e. leave Big Bird alone

149. In 1984, Newt said that he and his supporters may be "the real ____________."

a. Founding Fathers

b. right-wing hatchet men

c. Goldwater Girls

d. Reagan reactionaries

e. Gary Hart

150. Describing the reaction of Democrats to him, Newt said, "I clearly _________ them."

a. appall

b. terrorize

c. excite

d. fascinate

e. annoy

VII. THE WORLD ACCORDING TO NEWT

In January 1995, Newt gave a lecture entitled "From Virtuality to Reality" at a conference sponsored by his favorite think tank, the Progress and Freedom Foundation. Delivered to futurists, spiritualists, self-improvement experts, and "cyberspace cartographers," Newt's talk was peppered with such conservative-futurist terms as "byte-cities," "brain lords," and "cyberpolitics."

Here are some key lines from Newt's speech: "If you think about the notion that the great challenge of our lifetime is first to imagine a future that is worth spending our lives getting to, and then, because of the technologies and the capabilities we have today, to get it up to sort of a virtual state, although that's done in terms of actual levels of sophistication, all that's done in your mind. Most studies of leadership argue that leaders actually are acting out past decisions. The problem when you get certainty with great leaders is that they have already thoroughly envisioned the achievement, and now it's just a matter of implementation. And so it's very different. And so in a sense, virtuality at the mental level is something I think you find in most leadership over historical periods. But in addition, the thing I want to talk about today and that I find fascinating is that we are not in a new place; it is just harder and harder and harder to avoid the place we are."

Now, understanding the world according to Newt may seem extremely difficult. However, it's actually just a matter of comprehending five easy concepts.

The first Newt notion is *waves*. According to Newt (borrowing from Alvin and Heidi Toffler), there have been three waves in human history: (1) the conversion from a hunter-gatherer to an agricultural society; (2) b the Industrial Revolution; and (3) the Information Revolution.

Concept number two: *a model for change.* Newt often quotes a prototype he says was developed by Alfred P. Sloan (former president of General Motors) and General George C. Marshall: "Real change occurs at the levels of vision and strategy. It is important to realize that vision must precede strategy, strategy precede operations, and operations precede tactics."

Newt's third vital idea: *the five pillars of American civilization.* They are: (1) personal strength; (2) free enterprise; (3) the spirit of invention and discovery; (4) quality; and (5) the lessons of American history.

The fourth idea in the Newtonian world: *transformation.* Newt says that "there are five transformations that are unavoidable if we are going to be a healthy society": (1) "from a second-wave mechanical bureaucratic model to a third-wave information model"; (2) "from a national economy to a world economy model"; (3) "from a welfare state to an opportunity society, because the Great Society experiment has failed totally"; (4) "from the counterculture and elites to a revitalization of American culture and civilization"; and (5) "from a professional politician class to a citizen-activist-leader system." In Newt's view, if all five transformations don't happen, "we don't make the successful transition into twenty-first-century America."

Newt idea number five is *staying inside the triangle.* The October 1989 issue of *Esquire* reports that in 1985 Newt "sat eating lunch in the Members' Dining Room, grabbed a napkin, and drew a triangle, labeling the sides 'reality,' 'personal lives,' and 'people's lives.' He explained, 'All successful politicians have to stay inside the triangle.'"

Newt's election as Speaker created a Newt World Order. Responsible citizens should learn everything they can about Newt's perspective on life. In this chapter, you'll be asked about Newt's views on space travel, civilization, history, the future, the counterculture, Washington, the welfare state, Woody Allen, and dumb rules. And remember: stay within the triangle.

151. What has Newt called the Food and Drug Administration?

- **a.** "Foodah"
- **b.** "It's home to thousands of drug users. A senior law enforcement official told me that one-quarter of the FDA staff has done drugs in the last five years."
- **c.** "Why can't they come up with food that won't make me so pudgy?"
- **d.** "a Stalinist agency"
- **e.** "run by Dr. Kevorkian's pals"

152. According to Newt, "___________ kills more people in a year than private business."

- **a.** The welfare state
- **b.** Ted Kennedy's driving
- **c.** The liberal elite media
- **d.** Jeffrey Dahmer
- **e.** An orphanage

153. According to Newt, what happens each year in Washington, D.C.?

- **a.** Lobbyists make nine hundred successful bribes to Democratic Congressmen.
- **b.** Marion Barry does one hundred lines of coke.
- **c.** Ross Perot shows up in alligator shoes and offers to look under the hood.
- **d.** Mind-numbed dittoheads invade the IRS demanding complete refunds.
- **e.** About eight hundred babies are thrown away.

154. According to Newt, "What's wrong with saying that when school's out, ____________"

- **a.** you can marry your high school math teacher?
- **b.** you can use the football field for target practice with your assault rifle?
- **c.** you can hire kids as young as twelve or thirteen?
- **d.** you can smoke marijuana on the playground, so long as you know how to inhale?
- **e.** you can pay somebody to do your sex ed homework?

155. What did Newt say about the 1985 summit meeting between Ronald Reagan and Mikhail Gorbachev?

a. "Why is Ronald Reagan playing footsie with the Communists?"

b. "Mr. Bedtime for Bonzo Meets Mr. Hammer and Sickle on His Forehead."

c. "A complete waste of time. Gorbachev doesn't have any power. Reagan should be holding a summit meeting with *me.*"

d. "It was completely unfair—a mental midget vs. a Communist giant."

e. "The most dangerous summit for the West since Munich."

156. According to Newt, Woody Allen's romance with twenty-one-year-old Soon-Yi Previn (the adoptive daughter of his former companion, Mia Farrow) "_____________."

a. qualifies Woody for membership in the Bill Clinton Seduction Club

b. fits the Democratic platform

c. makes me wanna holler

d. is really impressive for an old Jewish guy. Way to go, Woodman!

e. is as bad as Clarence Thomas talking about pubic hair on Coke cans

157. Which of the following is one of Newt's applause lines from his standard speech?

a. "Segregation today, segregation tomorrow, segregation forever!"

b. "The Democratic Party is pathetic, corrupt, insipid, permissive, destructive, shallow, and incompetent. Bill Clinton is perfect as their leader."

c. "Sure, I'm a deeply flawed person. I've done drugs, dodged the draft, abandoned my sick wife, been sued for alimony payments, and defamed lots of honorable people. But I believe in redemption. If I can restore myself, I can restore America."

d. "It is impossible to maintain civilization with twelve-year-olds having babies, fifteen-year-olds killing each other, with seventeen-year-olds dying of AIDS, and eighteen-year-olds ending up with diplomas when they can't even read."

e. "Extremism in the defense of liberty is no vice; moderation in the pursuit of justice is no virtue."

158. According to Newt, "Most people don't realize it's illegal to __________ in public schools."

a. pray

b. show up at the senior prom without a date

c. watch 'Melrose Place'

d. refuse to do your algebra homework

e. sniff glue

159. What does Newt propose to help poor Americans?

a. paying every poor person one hundred dollars to join the Republican Party

b. giving them each a copy of *Think and Grow Rich*

c. providing tax credits for purchasing a laptop computer

d. establishing a federal dating service for single parents

e. providing free sterilization for poor women

160. How did Newt describe New York City?

a. "Woody Allen's dating haven"

b. "It's more responsible than any other city for the decline of American civilization. It's home to Peter Jennings, Dan Rather, Tom Brokaw, and Howard Stern—plus all their pornographic pals."

c. "A black guy was mayor. I thought that was supposed to solve everything."

d. "a strong argument for sawing off the Eastern seaboard and letting it float into the ocean"

e. a city of "AIDS activists, left-wing environmentalists, ultra-feminists, unilateral disarmers, and random professional politicians"

161. What does Newt call "the dumbest rule I've ever seen"?

a. the rule barring elected officials from teaching at Georgia public colleges

b. the rule enacted by House Republicans restricting his Speakership to eight years

c. the rule that says you can't marry your high school math teacher

d. the rule that says you can't have accept a mountain of cash from a foreign businessman thinly disguised as a book deal

e. the rule that says that the president, rather than the Speaker, gets to sign or veto legislation

162. According to Newt, "You have to say to the counterculture: _______________."

a. It's not the Age of Aquarius anymore. It's the Age of Newt

b. Thanks for the memories. It was real, babe

c. Pot: yes; acid: no

d. I've burned my mood rings!

e. Nice try. You failed. You're wrong

163. Which two of the following descriptions of the Democratic Party has Newt made?

a. "Democratic leaders are sick. They are so consumed by their own power, by a Mussolini-like ego, that their willingness to run over normal human beings and to destroy honest institutions is unending."

b. "They will do anything to stop us. They will use any tool. There is no grotesquerie, no distortion, no dishonesty too great for them to come after us."

c. "It certainly makes sense that a jackass is their symbol."

d. "They're the Democrat Party, not the Democratic Party. I learned that from Bob Dole. I know they officially changed their name in 1948, and I know it makes us sound stupid, but we say it that way to annoy them. It's like Bush deliberately mispronouncing 'Saddam Hussein,' just to piss him off. My goal in life is to piss off the Democrats."

e. "Gary Hart, Ted Kennedy, Chuck Robb—they're the original Bachelors III."

164. What did Newt describe as "Very, very dumb"?

a. a typical "Seinfeld" episode

b. his own dissertation

c. the possibility that President Clinton might try to obstruct the Republican agenda

d. the idea that Senator Phil Gramm would make a good president

e. Dan Quayle's analysis of "Murphy Brown"

165. According to Newt, "A healthy society starts out saying, ________________."

a. 'hey, dudes—let's party!'

b. 'life is hard'

c. 'Kato Kaelin: role model for our nation's youth'

d. 'get yourself two heterosexual parents with jobs, or it's Orphanage City'

e. 'here's a TV. Start wasting your life'

166. In 1989, how did Newt describe the House of Representatives?

a. "party town, USA"

b. "guys and dolls"

c. "dumb and dumber"

d. "a corrupt institution"

e. "Foley's fat farm"

167. In Newt's view, "__________ is to blame for most of the current, major diseases which have struck this society."

- **a.** That bitch Hillary Clinton
- **b.** Ross Perot
- **c.** The Left
- **d.** Roseanne
- **e.** Rupert Murdoch

168. In Newt's view, what may become "commonplace" in the future?

- **a.** "having a hypocritical windbag as Speaker of the House"
- **b.** "weirdos taking potshots at the White House"
- **c.** "pornographic movies financed by Senator Gramm"
- **d.** "men giving birth"
- **e.** "spending a week's vacation on a space station or a honeymoon on the moon"

169. How does Newt classify most experiences?

- **a.** either neat or weird
- **b.** either orgasmic or depressing
- **c.** either heavenly or satanic
- **d.** either black or white
- **e.** either revolutionary or reactionary

170. How does Newt characterize his philosophy toward government?

- **a.** "To each according to their need, from each according to their ability."
- **b.** "I don't mind paying taxes. With them I buy civilization."
- **c.** "I'm for a limited government, but a very strong limited government."
- **d.** "The rights of Republicans always outweigh the rights of Democrats."
- **e.** "My life, my liberty, and the pursuit of my happiness."

171. "Gingrich" is not in the spell-check dictionary for Microsoft Word for Windows 6.0. However, what word does the dictionary suggest as an alternative?

a. "hypocrite"

b. "blockhead"

c. "grinch"

d. "jingoish"

e. "ostrich"

172. What did Newt say about President Clinton's "Americorps" national service program?

a. "I am totally opposed to national service. It is coerced voluntarism. It's gimmickry."

b. "Anything that uses tax dollars to help people, I'm against."

c. "If it wasn't Clinton's idea, I'd be for it."

d. "If somebody wants to be a volunteer, I could use some help writing a couple of books."

e. "We've already got a national service corps. It's called the marines."

173. At a 1989 Conservative Leadership Conference, what recommendation on education policy did Newt make?

- **a.** giving each student an "A" in every subject, to improve self-esteem
- **b.** offering kids one hundred dollars to read fifty books a year and paying them to skip grades
- **c.** abolishing social studies, since "history is bunk"
- **d.** requiring that a prayer be recited before every math test
- **e.** abolishing physics and chemistry, because "only Asians can understand that stuff"

174. How did Newt characterize the Vietnam War?

- **a.** "a weird psychedelic trip"
- **b.** "Forrest Gump's finest hour"
- **c.** "I really don't remember. I was high at the time."
- **d.** "the right battle at the right time"
- **e.** "Didn't Rambo look great?"

175. In May 1984, Newt stood in the well of the House to speak on foreign policy. Which four of the following charges against Democrats did he make?

a. He called them "blind to communism."

b. He threatened to "file charges" against ten Democrats for a letter they wrote to Nicaraguan leader Daniel Ortega.

c. He accused one Democrat of placing "Communist propaganda" in the Speaker's lobby.

d. He called them "fellow travelers on the Havana/Beijing/Moscow shuttle."

e. He said, "Democrats don't even bother to learn foreign languages. How are they going to understand Latin America if they don't learn Latin?"

f. He said that Democrats opposing aid to the Nicaraguan contras "could wear an 'I despise America' button."

Answers and Their Sources

1. d Dale Russakoff, "He Knew What He Wanted," *The Washington Post*, December 18, 1994, p. A28.

2. a *The Washington Post*, December 18, 1994, p. A28.

3. e David Osborne, "Newt Gingrich: Shining Knight of the Post-Reagan Right," *Mother Jones*, November 1984, p. 16. As Speaker, Newt has in fact made the argument in answer D. The "Doonesbury" cartoon of February 28, 1995, satirizes Newt (as a cherry bomb) saying, "Dating in high school is simply out of control. If taxpayers knew what was going on, they'd be *outraged!*"

4. **All of the statements are real:**
a, b, c, d, e: *Mother Jones*, November 1984, pp. 19-20.
f: David Beers, "Master of Disaster," *Mother Jones*, October 1989, p. 44.
g: Lois Romano, "Newt Gingrich: Maverick on the Hill," *The Washington Post*, January 3, 1985, p. B1.

Statement A was made by Chip Kahn, who ran two of Newt's campaigns, and has known him since 1968. Statement B was made by Chip's wife, Mary. Statements C, D, and E were made by L. H. Carter, who was one of Newt's closest friends and advisers until a falling out in 1979. Statement F was made by Lee Howell, Newt's first press aide. Statement G was made by then–congressman Vin Weber, a Minnesota Republican.

5. b Paul Grondahl, "Scientific Facts and Pointed Observations About Newts," *Santa Barbara News-Press*, December 18, 1994, p. G1.

6. c Mark Hosenball, "How 'Normal' is Newt?" *Newsweek*, November 7, 1994, p. 34.

7. e Dale Russakoff and Dan Balz, "Freshman Gingrich Made Majority a Goal," *The Washington Post*, December 19, 1994, p. A19.

8. c Bill Hewitt, Linda Kramer, and Sarah Slolnik, "Having Read George Bush's Lips and Believed, Newt Gingrich Says No to Taxes—And to the President," *People*, November 12, 1990, pp. 62-63. The movie, Newt says, "really drove into me a real sense that the highest purpose is to do your duty."

9. b *The Washington Post*, December 18, 1994, p. A28.

10. e *The Washington Post*, December 18, 1994, p. A1

11. c *The Washington Post*, December 18, 1994, p. A1.

12. d *The Washington Post*, December 18, 1994, p. A1.

13. a *Mother Jones*, November 1984, pp. 16-17. Journalist David Osborne reports the story as follows:

Like a number of his classmates, he also developed a crush on his math teacher. But unlike the other boys his age, Gingrich didn't leave it at that. She moved to Atlanta; he enrolled at Emory University. One day, Jackie recalls, there was a knock on her door, and there stood Gingrich, seven years her junior. She still remembers the conversation:

"I'm here," he announced.

"Yeah?"

"Yeah, I came. I'm here."

"He had made up his mind," she says with a smile. "We dated and went together for that year, his freshman year in school, and we got married the next June." Newt was always very "persistent, and persuasive."

14. e "Gingrich Says He Has a Ford," *The New York Times*, November 18, 1994, p. B8.

15. c Howard Fineman, "The Warrior," *Newsweek*, January 9, 1995, p. 30.

16. d *Newsweek*, January 9, 1995, p. 31.

17. a, c, f, g:
Gingrich's mom

b, d, e, h:
Clinton's mom
"Battle of the Moms," *Time*, January 16, 1995, p. 20.

18. d *Mother Jones*, November 1984, p. 19. Newt continued: "In fact I think they were sufficiently inconsistent that at one point in 1979 and 1980, I began to quit saying them in public. One of the reasons I ended up getting a divorce was that if I was disintegrating enough as a person that I could not say those things, then I needed to get my life straight, not quit saying them. And I think that literally was the crisis I came to. I guess I look back on it a little bit like somebody who's in Alcoholics Anonymous—it was a very, very bad period of my life, and it had been getting steadily worse. . . . I ultimately wound up at a point where probably suicide or going insane or divorce were the last three options."

19. e James Carney and Karen Tumulty, "Master of the House," *Time*, January 16, 1995, p. 29.

20. a *The Washington Post,* December 18, 1994, p. A28.

21. b "The Incumbent Party, The Party of Incumbents," *National Review,* June 30, 1989, pp. 14-15.

22. c *The Washington Post,* December 18, 1994, p. A28.

23. d Ann Devroy, "Clinton Consults a Gingrich Guru," *The Washington Post,* January 4, 1995, p. A1. Covey co-wrote one of the "readings" for Newt's college course, a chapter on "personal strength in American culture."

24. d *The Washington Post,* December 19, 1994, p. A1.

25. e "Mrs. Gingrich Echoes First Lady Comment," *The Los Angeles Times,* January 9, 1995, p. A13. This incident look on a life of its own. Many observers criticized Connie Chung for supposedly tricking Newt's mom into making the statement. Hillary responded by inviting Newt and his mom for a tour of the White House. President Clinton joked about the matter: "God knows what they could have gotten *my* mother to say." Jay Leno said this about Newt's week: "He started it with his 'Contract With America' and ended it with a contract on Connie Chung." Newt's mom said later on the syndicated TV program "American Journal," "What's all the fuss about? Because I said she was a bitch. And that's what all the pins are saying. Yes, she is."

26. e Weston Kosova, "The Elephant Man," *The New Republic,* November 7, 1994, p. 30.

27. c *Dissertation Abstracts,* University Microfilms, 1994. Gingrich, Newton Leroy. Tulane University. Degree: Ph.D. Date: 1971. p: 307.

28. a Eleanor Clift, "Now, A Whole Newt World," *Newsweek,* November 21, 1994, p. 40. *Chimpanzee Politics* is "a study of how raw power and bluster are used to gain ascendancy in the jungle."

29. e "Sayings of a Revolutionary," *Newsweek,* November 21, 1994, p. 40.

30. e Kathleen Q. Seelye, "Gingrich's Life: The Complications and Ideals," *The New York Times,* November 24, 1994, p. A1.

31. b Serge F. Kovaleski, "Gingrich Tells Publisher to Drop Bush Reference," *The Washington Post,* December 2, 1994, p. A1. A few months later, in a subsequent draft, Newt described the future president in more complimentary terms: "He had been one of the youngest flight leaders in the fleet, but by God if you needed someone to lead a group straight into enemy flak like they were on rails, he was your man." Maureen Dowd, "Tantalizing Advance Look at House Speaker's Prose," *The New York Times,* February 23, 1995, p. A11.

32. c, d, f, h, l, o, q
Adam Clymer, "Republicans All for One, and the One Is Gingrich," *The New York Times*, December 5, 1994, p. A1.

33. d *The Washington Post*, December 2, 1994, p. A26.

34. a *Time*, November 7, 1994, p. 31. This, in spite of the fact that Newt considers himself "the GOP advance man for the future."

35. c *Newsweek*, January 9, 1995, p. 33.

36. e *The Washington Post*, December 3, 1994, p. A1.

37. c *The Washington Post*, December 19, 1994, p. A18.

38. e *The New York Times*, November 23, 1994, p. A1. The book's plot concerns a boy's struggle to prove himself to his father—a cold, austere, overbearing military officer.

39. a *The Washington Post*, December 18, 1994, p. A1.

40. e *The Washington Post*, December 18, 1994, p. A1.

41. c *The Washington Post*, December 18, 1994, p. A29.

42. **Newt made all the statements.**
Melissa Healy, "Partisan Feud Erupts in House Over Gingrich Book Deal," *The Los Angeles Times*, January 19, 1995, p. A6. Newt's comments on gender prompted *The Washington Post* to sponsor a contest in which readers were invited to come up with "Gingrichisms," defined as "colorful if slightly Neanderthal explanations of the basic principles of life."

—The Winner (Greg Arnold, Herndon, Virginia): "Men are better decision makers than women. This capacity is developed at an early age during toilet training. Every time a man goes to the bathroom he makes a conscious decision to stand or sit. That trait is underdeveloped in women, who are always dithering over every little thing."

—First Runner-Up (Dave Yanchulis, Washington, D.C.): "Joan of Arc? Dead of infection. Look it up."

—Second Runner-Up (Mark Briscoe, Arlington, Virginia): "We should consider employing an entirely female navy, because a woman's anatomy makes her particularly well suited for use as a flotation device."

—Honorable Mention (Kim Patterson, Gaithersburg, Maryland): "Women are better at sweatshop work. Their perspiration doesn't smell as bad in close quarters and they like to sew clothes. Men need to work outside where they can sweat and urinate freely. Children can be kept in orphanages above the sweatshops."

—Honorable Mention (Rick Sasaki, Arlington, Virginia): "Bill Clinton is a Democrat. The Democrats are donkeys. That means he is an ass. I am a Republican. The Republicans are elephants. That means I have large genitals."

—Honorable Mention (Allen R. Breon, Columbia, Maryland): "T-shirts are a symbol of acceptance and honor. Bumper stickers are cold and hurt like crazy when you take them off."

"The Style Invitational: Report From Week 97," *The Washington Post*, February 12, 1995, p. F2.

43. d *Newsweek*, January 9, 1995, p. 31.

44. a *The Washington Post*, December 21, 1994, p. A19. Brinkley, though, does give Newt credit for not being "content to offer a conventional, conservative, grouchy message."

45. d Dan Balz, "The Latest on Gingrich," *The Washington Post*, February 5, 1995, p. A6. Jim Whitney, spokesman for the Democratic National Committee, said that "Newt Inc. is such a vast empire with so many tentacles that we decided it was useful to remind people of what was going on." Whitney said it was an effort "to be a little more aggressive" toward the opposition.

46. e *Newsweek*, January 9, 1995, p. 30. The book argues that some men both need and resent the presence of a dominating woman. "It's a wonder I'm not a psychological mess," Newt told a friend years ago.

47. e Nando Amabile, "A Normal American" (letter to the editor), *The New Republic*, December 12, 1994, p. 4. Amabile was Newt's high school sophomore English teacher.

48. d *The New Republic*, November 7, 1994, p. 29.

49. a "Excerpts From Gingrich's Speech on Party's Agenda for the 104th Congress," *The New York Times*, January 5, 1995, p. A23.

50. b Katharine Q. Seelye, "Gingrich Takes Capitol by Storm With Eye to History," *The New York Times*, January 5, 1995, p. A23.

51. d Elizabeth Shogren, "Gingrich Says He Opposes U.S. Version of 187," *The Los Angeles Times*, December 5, 1994, p. A13.

52. a Keith Bradsher, "Many White House Employees Used Drugs, Gingrich Asserts," *The New York Times*, December 5, 1995, p. A17.

53. d *The Washington Post*, November 10, 1994, p. A1. Answer B is from Mark Alan Stamaty, "Washingtoon," *Time*, January 30, 1995, p. 17.

54. e *Newsweek*, November 21, 1994, p. 40.

55. d Thomas B. Rosenthal, "It's Rush Night for GOP's Lawmakers-in-Waiting," *The Los Angeles Times*, December 11, 1994, p. A41.

56. d David Van Biema, "The Storm Over Orphanages," *Time*, December 12, 1994, p. 58.

57. c Carl Mollins, "Tough-Talking Georgian," *Maclean's*, November 7, 1994, p. 39.

58. d *Maclean's*, November 7, 1994, p. 39.

59. a Fred Barnes, "The Odd Couple," *The New Republic*, November 28, 1994, p. 16.

60. c Adam Clymer, "G.O.P. Celebrates Its Sweep to Power; Clinton Vows to Find Common Ground," *The New York Times*, November 9, 1994, p. B5.

61. b *Time*, November 7, 1994, p. 32.

62. b Ann Devroy and Charles R. Babcock, "Gingrich's New Challenger," *The Washington Post*, March 6, 1994, p. A12.

63. e Amy B. Bernstein and Peter W. Bernstein, editors, *Quotations From Speaker Newt: The Little Red, White, and Blue Book of the Republican Revolution* (New York: Workman Publishing, 1995), p. 75. Newt continued: "We encourage you to be neat, obedient, and loyal and faithful, and all those Boy Scout words, which would be great around the camp fire, but are lousy in politics."

64. f *The New York Times*, November 9, 1994, p. B2.

65. c *The New York Times*, November 24, 1994, p. A1.

66. a, b, d, f, h, j, k, l, m

Serge F. Kolaleski, "Gingrich's Guru: Corporate Psychotherapist Enlisted to Shape Message," *The Washington Post*, December 8, 1994, p. A1. Similarly, Frank Luntz, Newt's pollster, had some rhetorical suggestions for Newt in a January 1995 memo. Luntz's advice was that "orphanages" are out, "foster homes" are in; cutting individual federal "programs" is out, cutting "bureaucrats or bureaucracies" is in; and "devolution" is out, "sending Washington home" is in. Luntz also argued that the federal budget debate should be described in terms of "the

American dream" and "our children's future," and that "nothing resonates like 'work.'" Jeanne Cummings, "Gingrich's 'Dialogues' With Public," *The San Francisco Chronicle*, February 6, 1995, p. A7.

67. c Katherine Q. Seelye, "Gingrich First Masterminded the Media and Then Rose to be King of the Hill," *The New York Times*, December 13, 1994, p. A20.

68. e *Newsweek*, November 7, 1994, p. 34.

69. d "Gingrich Vows $2,000 for Barney, Big Bird," *The Los Angeles Times*, January 3, 1995, p. A2. In making the pledge, Newt said, "Big Bird makes money. Barney makes money. These are profit-making centers, they would survive fine. . . . I understand why the elite wants money [for public TV], but I think they ought to be honest. These are a bunch of rich, upper-class people who want their toy to play with."

70. c *Newsweek*, January 9, 1995, p. 33.

71. a *Mother Jones*, October 1989, p. 42.

72. d Adam Clymer, "House Revolutionary," *The New York Times Magazine*, August 23, 1992, p. 47.

73. a *Time*, January 9, 1995, p. 24. The bill was H.R. 4286, the National Space and Aeronautics Policy Act of 1981. Title IV, Government of Space Territories, "sets forth provisions for the government of space colonies, including constitutional protections, the right to self-government, and admission to statehood."

74. e Adam Myerson, "Miracle Whip: Can Newt Gingrich Save the Bush Presidency?" *Policy Review*, Winter 1991, p. 14.

75. d Campaign flyer (Ingram Library, West Georgia College, 1978). Cited in *Quotations From Speaker Newt*, p. 13.

76. c "Viewpoint," *US News and World Report*, November 28, 1994, p. 47. Newt was apologizing for calling the Clinton administration "the enemy of normal Americans."

77. a "Welcome to the Gingrich Nation," *US News and World Report*, November 21, 1994, p. 44. Newt continued: "We are at the end of an era. And some people have to form the bridge into the new one."

78. e Maureen Dowd, "Gingrich, Now a Round Peg, Seeks to Smooth the Edges," *The New York Times*, December 9, 1994, p. A30.

79. d *The New York Times*, November 24, 1994, p. A1.

80. d *Mother Jones*, November 1984, p. 16.

81. c *Newsweek*, January 9, 1995, p. 28.

82. a Nicholas Lemann, "'Conservative Opportunity Society,'" *The Atlantic Monthly*, May 1985, p. 25. Answer D is based on a statement made by Texas congressman Dick Armey.

83. c Katharine Q. Seelye, "Saving Money in Congress: Dump the House Historian and Hire a New One," *The New York Times*, January 8, 1995, p. 10.

84. e *Mother Jones*, October 1989, p. 42.

85. a Ronald Brownstein, "Will Gingrich Learn to Dampen the Fiery Rhetoric Before He Combusts?" *The Los Angeles Times*, January 30, 1995, p. A5. Bob Dole said this about Newt's problems: "You live by the sword, you die by the sword in this town."

86. e *Mother Jones*, October 1989, p. 44.

87. d Dan Balz and Serge F. Kovalski, "In Bush Budget Revolt, Gingrich Took the Reins," *The Washington Post*, December 21, 1994, p. A18.

88. a *The New York Times Magazine*, August 23, 1992, p. 41.

89. c *Newsweek*, January 9, 1995, p. 28. According to Howard Fineman, Newt's commonality with de Gaulle is their belief in nationalism and technology. However, Fineman notes, de Gaulle, "a symbol of freedom, ended up an autocrat, a man behind a gilded desk who thought that only he could see the future of his country, and who saw his worst enemies among his fellow countrymen. Another American who admired de Gaulle was Richard Nixon. And we all know what happened to him."

90. c *People*, November 12, 1990, p. 64.

91. d "Bringing Down the House," *Time*, November 7, 1994, p. 31.

92. d Michael Kramer, "Newt's Believe It Or Not," *Time*, December 19, 1994, p. 44.

93. a *The Washington Post*, December 21, 1994, p. A18.

94. c *The Washington Post*, January 3, 1985, p. B2.

95. d Emma Edmunds, "Cool Hand Newt," *Atlanta Magazine*, January 1990, p. 47. Newt continued: "I am not in any significant way an extremist. I was a backbencher who knew that in order to be effective, you had to use certain techniques. . . ."

96. a Peter Osterlund, "A Capitol Chameleon: What Will Newt Gingrich Do Next?" *The Los Angeles Times Magazine*, August 25, 1991, p. 37.

97. e *The Los Angeles Times Magazine*, August 25, 1991, p. 40.

98. b *The Los Angeles Times Magazine*, August 25, 1991, p. 37.

99. d *The Washington Post*, January 3, 1985, p. B1.

100. a Eric Schmitt, "Republicans Finding Dissension in Ranks on Military Issues," *The New York Times*, January 29, 1995, p. 9.

101. e *The New Republic*, November 28, 1994, p. 15.

102. c *The New Republic*, November 28, 1994, p. 15.

103. c *Time*, December 19, 1994, cover.

104. e Kevin Phillips, "Fat-Cat Revolutionaries," *The Los Angeles Times*, December 18, 1994, p. M1.

105. d Kevin Phillips, "Capital Mayhem," *The Los Angeles Times*, January 8, 1995, p. M1. The continuation of Phillips's comments on Dole: "He's now viewed as a sort of grizzled Kansas high school principal, separating ninth-grade Republicans in the House from Democratic sophomores in the White House. Since this three-way comparison began in the polls six weeks ago, the Bobster's numbers have climbed like Jack's beanstalk."

106. c Sidney Blumenthal, "The Politics of Hope ('Boys Town') vs. the Politics of Fear ('Disclosure')," *The Los Angeles Times*, December 18, 1994, p. M2.

107. a "Viewpoint," *US News and World Report*, November 21, 1994, p. 34.

108. b Howard Fineman, "Clinton Values Blowout," *Newsweek*, December 19, 1994, p. 26.

109. e *National Review*, June 30, 1989, p. 14.

110. d *People*, November 12, 1990, p. 63.

111. d *Esquire*, November 1994, p. 52.

112. d Howard Kurtz, "Scourge of the GOP Whip: Gingrich Dukes it Out With the Elite Media," *The Washington Post*, November 16, 1994, p. B1.

113. c "Newt Gingrich, Authoritarian," *The New York Times*, November 13, 1994, section 4, p. 14. The editorial continued: "In Newt's 'Retro-World,'" intellectual dissent is "unpatriotic and infuriating."

114. a *The Washington Post*, November 16, 1994, p. B1.

115. e Tony Kornheiser, "How the Gingrich Stole Christmas," *The Washington Post*, November 13, 1994, p. F1.

116. c Maureen Dowd, "The 1994 Elections: The House. The Republican Leader," *The New York Times*, November 9, 1994, p. B2.

117. d "Jokes," *The Los Angeles Times*, January 6, 1995, p. E2.

118. a Katherine Q. Seelye, "Gingrich Used TV Skills to be King of the Hill," *The New York Times*, December 14, 1994, p. A16.

119. c David E. Rosenbaum, "A Republican Who Sees Himself as a Revolutionary on the Verge of Victory," *The New York Times*, July 24, 1994, p. 14.

120. b "Capital Gang," CNN, January 21, 1995.

121. d Molly Ivins, "Smart as a Shrub," *The Progressive*, May 1989, p. 40. Molly Ivins's statement in its entirety: "Newt Gingrich, now there's a gladsome tiding. Great hair, no integrity. He's the real Bob Forehead. The reason Republicans elected this repellant little demagogue to the whipship is that they thought it would annoy Democrats. That's the Donald Segretti school of politics. With any luck, Robert K. Dornan will be next." In 1992, Ivins called Newt "a thoroughly nasty man." ". . . Not Your Normal Smear," *The Washington Post*, August 26, 1992, p. A23. Answer E is an actual statement, from William Sternberg, "Housebreaker," *The Atlantic*, June 1993, p. 26. The statement begins, "To his detractors, Newt Gingrich is . . ."

122. e *Esquire*, November 1994, p. 51.

123. c *Time*, cover, November 7, 1994. Newt was also on the cover of *Time* on January 9, 1995, with the headline "King of the Hill."

124. d *The Los Angeles Times Magazine*, August 25, 1991, p. 42. Jim Tilden, a high school friend, described Newt as "a classic nerd. He had no taste in clothing."

125. b *The Washington Post*, January 3, 1985, p. B2.

126. e "Meet the Press," December 1, 1991. Cited in Tom Connor and Associates, *NewtWit! The Wit and Wisdom of Newt Gingrich* (New York: Doubleday, 1995), p. 24.

127. d Helen Dewar, "Republicans Wage Verbal Civil War," *The Washington Post*, November 19, 1984, p. A1. Years later, Newt said of Dole, "He's learning. He's maturing." "Right Makes Might," *Time*, November 21, 1994, p. 53.

128. a *Mother Jones*, October 1989, p. 29. Dole continued: "They think they can peddle the idea that they've taken over the party. Well, they aren't the Republican Party, and they aren't going to be."

129. d *The Washington Post*, December 18, 1994, p. A29.

130. c Ann Devroy, "Panetta Holds Gingrich's Words Against Him—And His Party," *The Washington Post*, December 6, 1994, p. A21.

131. a *Time*, November 21, 1994, p. 53.

132. e *People*, November 12, 1990, p. 64.

133. d *Newsweek*, January 9, 1995, p. 34.

134. b *Newsweek*, January 9, 1995, p. 34.

135. b *The New York Times*, December 8, 1994, p. 30.

136. a *The New York Times*, December 4, 1994, p. A17.

137. a *The New York Times*, July 24, 1994, p. 14.

138. e Peter Applebome, "Republican Leader Practices Nonchalance in Tough Campaign," *The New York Times*, November 7, 1994, p. A12.

139. b Maureen Dowd, "G.O.P. 's Rising Star Pledges to Right Wrongs of the Left," *The New York Times*, November 10, 1994, p. B3.

140. e Dale Russakoff, "Gingrich Lobs a Few More Bombs," *The Washington Post*, November 10, 1994, p. A1.

141. a, b, c, d, e:
apply to McGovern

f, g, h, i, j:
apply to Newt
George McGovern, "A Word From the Original McGovernick," *The Washington Post*, December 25, 1994, p. C2.

142. e *The New York Times Magazine*, August 23, 1992, p. 47. Obey continued: "Newt enjoys smearing people's character. He con tributes to the destruction of the body politic."

143. d Katharine Q. Seelye, "The 1994 Campaign: The Republicans," *The New York Times*, October 27, 1994, p. A1. Synar continued: "Newt is dangerous because he's smart, he's articulate, and he's in control of his party. There is no dissension, and his principle and philosophy are as flexible as necessary."

144. c Karen Tumulty, "Man With a Mission," *Time*, January 9, 1995, p. 32.

145. e Karen Merida, "Speaker's Dress-Up, Dress-Down Day," *The Washington Post*, January 5, 1995, p. A1. Answer A is from Maureen Dowd, "Speaking for House Speaker and Enjoying the Trappings," *The New York Times*, January 5, 1995, p. A24.

146. a Fred Barnes, "Rebel With a Cause," *USA Weekend*, January 20-22, 1995, p. 5.

147. b *USA Weekend*, January 20-22, 1995, p. 5. Wright continued: "Torpedoing Congress and blaming the Democrats has been his route to power."

148. e Richard L. Berke, "Displaying Unity, Democratic Party Installs Its Leaders," *The New York Times*, p. 15. At the same meeting, President Clinton said this about Newt and the Republicans: "It's a funny world, that world they're sketching. A world in which Big Bird is an elitist and right-wing media magnates are populists."

149. e *The Washington Post*, November 19, 1984, p. A5. What Newt meant is that, just like Gary Hart, he and his supporters could attract new voters to the Republican Party by advocating new ideas.

150. d Dan Balz, "The Whip Who Would Be Speaker: Gingrich Sees Role as 'Transformational,'" *The Washington Post*, October 20, 1994, p. A26.

151. d Paul Grondahl, *Santa Barbara News-Press*, December 18, 1994, p. G1.

152. a *Newsweek*, November 21, 1994, p. 40.

153. e John Leo, "Newt Must Remove Foot From Mouth, Use Head," *Santa Barbara News-Press*, December 18, 1994, p. G1.

154. c Walter Shapiro, "Newt to the Rescue!" *Esquire*, November 1994, p. 51.

155. e *The Washington Post*, October 20, 1994, p. A1.

156. b George F. Will, "Serious People Flinch . . ." *The Washington Post*, August 26, 1992, p. A23. Newt's quotation in its entirety: "I call this the Woody Allen plank. It's a weird situation, and it fits the Democratic Party platform perfectly. If a Democrat used the word 'family' to raise children in Madison Square Garden, half their party would have rebelled, and the other would not vote. Woody Allen had nonincest with his non-daughter because they were a nonfamily." Will commented: "That would cost Gingrich his reputation for seriousness if he had one, and it illustrates how cynicism at the top of the Republican ticket pervades the entire party."

157. d E.J. Dionne Jr., "The Gingrich Challenge," *The Washington Post*, November 15, 1994, p. A19.

158. a Laurie Goldstein, "Disciplining of Student Is Defended; Gingrich Said Prayer Brought Punishment," *The Washington Post*, December 6, 1994, p. A25.

159. c Michael Kinsley, "Let Them Eat Laptops," *The New Yorker*, January 23, 1995, pp. 6-7. Kinsley points out that implementing Newt's suggestion could cost forty billion dollars, since there are approximately forty million people below the poverty line, and laptops cost around one thousand dollars.

160. e *The Los Angeles Times Magazine*, August 25, 1991, p. 74.

161. a *The New York Times*, January 8, 1995, p. 10.

162. e Catherine S. Manegold, "Gingrich, Now a Giant, Aims at Great Society," *The New York Times*, November 12, 1994, p. 9. Jacob Weisberg notes that, "for Newt, *counterculture* is the all-purpose pejorative, one that applies not just to say, the Grateful Dead and the *Whole Earth Catalog*, but to Lyndon Johnson's Great Society, the black underclass he contends it created, and the students who opposed Johnson's war in Vietnam. He uses it to blanket the entire Clinton administration, on the basis of age and party affiliation. In Newt's speeches, *counterculture* stands as shorthand for sex, drugs, and even left-wing politics, a conservative fantasy of liberal licentiousness." Jacob Weisberg, "Decoding Newtspeak," *New York*, November 28, 1994, p. 28.

163. a, b *Mother Jones*, October 1989, p. 33; and Robert Shogan, "Embattled Gingrich Slams Critics of His Book Deal," *The Los Angeles Times*, January 21, 1995, p. A4.

164. c *The New York Times*, November 12, 1994, p. 9.

165. b *The Washington Post*, December 19, 1994, p. A1.

166. d John M. Barry, "Anatomy of a Smear," *Esquire*, October 1989, p. 216.

167. c *Mother Jones*, October 1989, p. 29.

168. e Newt Gingrich, "Window of Opportunity," *The Futurist*, June 1985, p. 10.

169. a *Time*, January 9, 1995, p. 23.

170. c *Time*, January 9, 1995, p. 24.

171. d "Spell Check," *Newsweek*, January 23, 1995, p. 8.

172. a Joe Klein, "Bowling for Virtue," *Newsweek*, January 23, 1995, p. 26.

173. b David Gross and David P. Hamilton, "All Rightniks," *The New Republic*, January 22, 1990, p. 14.

174. d *Esquire*, October 1989, p. 218.

175. a, b, c, f

A, B, C: *Mother Jones*, November 1984, p. 15. F: *The Los Angeles Times*, January 30, 1995, p. A5.

About the Author

Ted Rueter earned a Ph.D. in political science from the University of Wisconsin–Madison. He has taught at Middlebury College, Georgetown University, and Smith College. He lives in San Luis Obispo, California.

Rueter is the author of *Carter vs. Ford: The Counterfeit Debates of 1976, Teaching Assistant Strategies: An Introduction to College Teaching, The United States in the World Political Economy, The Minnesota House of Representatives and the Professionalization of Politics, The Politics of Race: African Americans and the Political System*, and *The Rush Limbaugh Quiz Book*. His articles have appeared in *The New York Times, The Boston Globe, PS: Political Science and Politics, World Politics, The Journal of Politics, The Journal of Post-Keynesian Economics, Perspectives on Political Science*, and *Computerworld*.